THE MONSTER INSIDE OF ME

BY RON CARTER
With Martin Phillips

Copyright © 2025 Ron Carter

All rights reserved

No part of this book may be reproduced, or stored in a retrieval system, or transmitted in any form or by any means, electronic, mechanical, photocopying, recording, or otherwise, without express written permission of the publisher.

ISBN: 9798283937540

Cover design by: Art Painter
Library of Congress Control Number: 2018675309
Printed in the United States of America

I owe an immeasurable debt of gratitude to my ghostwriter, Martin Phillips, without whom this book would not have come to life. Martin is the kindest and most talented person I know, bringing his extraordinary gifts as a freelance journalist to this project. Having operated worldwide, he has covered all aspects of life with his insightful journalism, and his ability to capture my story with such depth and sensitivity has been remarkable. I extend my deepest gratitude to the Department of Veterans Affairs (VA) and the countless dedicated professionals who tirelessly serve veterans. It pains me to hear the VA unfairly labelled as "terrible." Yes, the VA is a vast and complex system, often tricky to navigate, and, like any organization, it has individuals with challenging attitudes - such personalities exist everywhere. Additionally, the VA staff skilfully manage interactions with veterans, some of whom can be quite gruff, with remarkable patience and care. I am profoundly thankful for the VA. Their support was nothing short of lifesaving. Had my trauma occurred outside the military, I would be left grappling with PTSD with much less assistance. The benefits and care provided by the VA are extraordinary, and I will forever cherish the compassion and support I have received. I also wish to express heartfelt thanks to my family and friends who have stood by me through every trial. The past few years have been profoundly isolating, and the unwavering presence of my loved ones has been a lifeline. Sharing my story cost me many friendships, particularly with lifelong male friends, making the loyalty of those who remained even more precious. Above all, I thank God Almighty for granting me life and the resilience to endure its challenges, enabling me to now support others. God's plan may not always align with our own, but it is always purposeful.

CONTENTS

Title Page
Copyright
Dedication
Author's note   3
Prologue   7
Chapter One   13
Chapter Two   21
Chapter Three   30
Chapter Four   37
Chapter Five   42
Chapter Six   46
Chapter Seven   54
Chapter Eight   62
Chapter Nine   71
Chapter Ten   77
Chapter Eleven   84
Chapter Twelve   90
Chapter Thirteen   97
Chapter Fourteen   102
Chapter Fifteen   111
Chapter Sixteen   113

Chapter Seventeen	118
Chapter Eighteen	124
Chapter Nineteen	128
Chapter Twenty	134
Afterword	141
Appendix i	144
Appendix ii	154
My conclusions:	160
About The Author	163
About The Author	165

THE MONSTER INSIDE OF ME

AUTHOR'S NOTE

For 35 years I kept what was done to me in the Army a deeply buried secret. I couldn't stand the shame and the torment of facing up to it when it happened and I certainly haven't felt in the intervening decades that anyone else would understand what I had suffered. So I locked what happened to my 19-year-old self in the cage of my subconscious, out of harm's way. Except that the harm had already been done and would keep being done all the while that it was silently, corrosively, eating away at me, shaping my entire adult life without me even realizing it. For 35 years. Never breathing a word to a living soul. In most of that time I have nevertheless been the person I want to be: friendly, caring, funny, successful, but the monster was always inside of me, ready to rear its ugly head should the red mist descend. And when it did, people got hurt - me and my loved ones included. For all those years I never recognized the cause of my monster. I thought – I hoped - that I had left the sexual trauma that I suffered far behind me, in the past, never to be mentioned again, but all the while it was controlling me, making me hyper-vigilant, heightening my fight-or-flight reflexes, exaggerating my sense of injustice, poisoning any feelings of trust and making me determined to be someone who no one would ever mess with again, however much that meant unleashing the monster from time to time. While the 19-year-old me was still locked in that cage, the adult me was getting lots of tattoos, working out constantly, honing my fighting skills, and carrying a gun, determined that no one would EVER touch me again without me allowing them to do so, and that if someone tried then either they'd die or I would! And that's a terrible, energy-sapping, black and white way to look at life, but that is what that single, devastating incident did to me. Hurt people hurt other people.

Eventually, recently, the truth did emerge and I was diagnosed with Post Traumatic Stress Disorder, but while that means I can now get treatment for my depression and try to finally come to terms with what I suffered, I am left with an aching, debilitating feeling of loss. I look back and mourn the 35 years I lived with untreated PTSD and lament how much better my life could have been had this crime not been committed against me, or had I got help sooner, and I have to admit it enrages me. It frustrates me, too, that I cannot remember with any clarity the exact details surrounding what happened to me. That is because I tried so hard and for so long to forget it. It is also part of the PTSD. You don't remember things and your brain doesn't want you to remember those things. It absolutely protects you by shutting you off from it, but to have those details might help me to understand and to rationalize it, and I can't, so I will describe in this book, as best I can, what happened to me, for the sake of the narrative, but many of the details will be pure speculation, or based on very hazy memory. The trouble at the time was that - and this is so common - I thought that I was one of the only ones that this stuff had happened to, but it happens to thousands of our young men and women soldiers every single year and it's scandalous. Thousands upon thousands of parents entrust their children to the military and I was one of those kids who signed up early for the delayed entry system. I readily volunteered to put my life on the line - in the meat grinder that is the infantry - knowing that I could get killed, and I was ready to take that chance, to be turned into one of the military's killing machines, but they don't tell the kids or their parents that the military is full of people who should look after them but who are in fact predators. You won't see the recruiting billboard that promises: "Join the Army, See the world. Learn new skills. And be raped!"

There is an epidemic of Military Sexual Trauma within our

armed forces. Nearly one in every ten women in the military and one in every 66 men has suffered MST. With 1.4 million personnel in the US military, that's more than 36,000 men and women who suffer sexual assault each year. Most assaults are by people of higher rank than the victims and the vast majority – around three-quarters – are not reported. I never reported my rape. Since I have been diagnosed, I have met so many other victims of MST, and their stories are so horribly similar. And it's not new. It's been going on, unaddressed, for generations. My therapists have told me of 75-year-old veterans coming forward, talking for the first time in their lives of how they were raped in Vietnam, 55 years ago, by men on their own side. It is a horrific fact that, in America, anywhere between 22 and 44 veterans a day take their own lives, depending on which figures you go by, and I believe that a significant number of those 22-a-day are people who have experienced MST. I draw no distinction between male victims and female victims. They have all suffered an appalling crime. But men are raised in a way that we don't talk about it. Like me, they hide behind foolish pride or fear of embarrassment and it destroys them. Or they kill themselves. And it has got to stop. I can't go back 35 years; I can't recover what I have lost, but I want some good to come out of the trauma I have been through so I want to spend what's left of the rest of my life advocating, teaching, getting young men to talk about what has been done to them, and getting them to get help. I don't know if I personally will ever get justice for what I have been through. I haven't decided yet whether to name the bastard who did what he did to me. As I sit here and write this now, I am still considering naming him later in this book. I might not. I might find the strength to name him in court. I might not. But far more important to me is getting young men who are abused - in the military or otherwise - to speak up. I know it's not easy. I would rather have died than say what happened to me. I very nearly did, more than once, at my own hand, and that's not the worst of the hurt that my MST has caused. Getting my PTSD diagnosis has been a blessing and a curse – a curse because I can now look back and say, "Goddamn it! I wish I'd have said something earlier." I don't want other young men to have their lives ruined by what-ifs. We have got to stop them killing themselves over something that should not have happened to them and was never their fault.

PROLOGUE

Even now I'm not sure why I was feeling so fragile that day. Nor did I have any idea of the dam of my emotions that was about to burst so dramatically. I certainly could not have guessed how my life was teetering on the edge of a precipice when I set out that morning, but it was and I will always be grateful to those who stopped me taking the next step. They saved my life.

It's a fairly short drive from my home in Bend, Oregon, to the city's Mountain View district and I was feeling OK, I thought, as I hit the road. The soldier within me was on duty as usual, of course, watching my mirrors intently as I gunned the V8 engine of my Toyota Tundra pick-up and eased through the traffic on NE 27th Street, but I was reasonably calm as I checked there was no-one on my tail or threatening to cut me off. Satisfied that my route was clear, I turned off onto NE Courtney Drive, pulled into the parking lot, found a bay near the exit with no other vehicles next to me and switched off the ignition. I was early for my appointment so I just sat there for a period staring at the newish, two-story building in front of me and gathering my thoughts, rehearsing in my head what I might be asked and how I would respond. I don't know why. It was just an annual check-up with the doctor, after all. No big deal. Physically I was in great shape. I always have been. I pride myself on the fitness that has been a part of who I am since long before I was in the Army and that I have maintained ever since. And outwardly there was nothing wrong with my mental state. Nothing that I could put my finger on, at least. My relationship with my on-off partner had been rocky, for sure, but it was fine at the time; my business was going well and things were certainly better than a year before when my staffing agency was still new and when I was dead broke and borrowing money for gas from my sister. That was when I decided to visit a doctor for a check-up for the first time in a long time but couldn't afford one. Look, I am proud of my military service and I will always be proud to call myself a veteran but I had previously avoided the 'VA' – facilities provided by the Department for Veterans Affairs – because I had heard terrible stories about them and, to be frank, I had never been aware of needing them. At that moment in time, however, without a spare dime to pay for medical treatment, I did need them, which is how I came to sign up. Despite Bend having a population of more than 100,000, it does not have a VA hospital, but the VA Outpatient Clinic, in the medical zone on the east side of town, is a decent sized facility, clean and airy, with friendly staff who are passionate about what they do for veterans. So, having wandered in due to financial hardship, I had been met by a guy who asked me how much money I made and, since I was pretty much making zero money at the time, he coded me for free medical help. Roll forward a year and my finances were much improved but I was back for my annual check-up. If I felt slightly uneasy that morning then that was nothing out of the ordinary. Being wary, constantly on my guard, forever working hard to give the appearance that I was not someone to trifle with… that was situation normal for me. I didn't like it but I had long since grown used to it. Dark thoughts were never too far away, although I had none that day, or none that I was aware of. And besides, it was a beautiful spring morning in Bend, typical for the high desert. The air was cool but the harsh overnight chill had gone and it felt mild. The carefully landscaped trees and shrubs around the neatly arranged facilities in the medical zone glistened with the moisture of thawed frost and, perfectly reflected in the VA clinic's many windows, were the distant Cascade Mountains set in a flawless blue sky. The only clouds gathering – brooding, stormy clouds – were in my head, though at that moment I didn't realize it. You see, most of the time I'm a pretty jovial, pleasant, loving, caring person, but there have been too many times in my adult life when I would lose my mind, either hurting people or myself or winding up in jail. Or all three. I call it my monster – a red rage that erupts without warning and is totally out of character. And, yes, in my early forties I had attempted suicide. With two broken marriages in quick succession, and facing the loss of all my assets tied up in the million-dollar dream home I had built on the back of many years of hard work, my life had been at rock bottom. It was only the thought of my son that had pulled me back from the brink on that occasion. Having failed to kill myself, I had done a quick online search for psychiatrists and picked one of the first I came across. She basically said there was nothing much wrong with me, prescribed me some pills and sent me on my way. I hated the way the anti-depressants made me feel so I was off them in in less than two weeks and, thank God, I had had no suicidal thoughts since. I wasn't in that same dark place now, so why did I feel kind of strange? After a while I got out of the car, checked all around me, then walked to the clinic entrance and up to the front reception desk. I announced my arrival for my appointment and I was directed to wait in one of those small rooms where they sit you to take your blood pressure and vitals while you wait for the doctor to see you. I still felt sort of OK, ready for the examination and to answer the doctor's questions. But that's when everything changed.

"How are you Ron?' said Garnie-Jo Carter-Powell, my physician assistant, as she walked into the room with a cheerful smile. I opened my mouth to reply but nothing came out. Tears filled my eyes and then I just started crying. The harder I tried to speak, the more the tears came until I was sobbing uncontrollably in just the craziest way. I had never cried like that in front of anyone in all my 54 years, but I could not stop. "Well, I can see you're not good," she said. I just shook my head because I still couldn't talk. I have never felt so overwhelmed by emotion in my life. I just sat there, crying, unable to do anything about it. "Look,

I'm going to call upstairs to see if someone is free to have a talk with you," said Garnie-Jo. I could only nod, and carried on crying. A quick call confirmed that there was a psychiatrist available and within ten minutes Stacy Dodd had dropped everything to come to see me, though I was still incoherent, gulping for breath as tears ran down my cheeks. I must have cried solidly for 30 minutes or more until Stacy finally got me calmed down. When I could finally talk I told her I was exhausted and no longer wanted to live the way I was. "I can't fight another day," I sobbed. "I'm just so tired from all the fighting." Then she told me: "We're going to have you take some tests." My eyes were red and sore and I felt totally drained, but I was finally composed enough to respond when she came back with some forms to fill in. They were a series of questions which didn't take me too long to answer. Then, after reading through what I had written, Stacy put down the forms, looked up and told me: "You have severe depression and PTSD." My 'fighting', she explained, was hyper-vigilance, typical of PTSD sufferers. While most people's fight-or-flight dial is usually set around '2' – ready to rise in the event of a sudden threat - mine was constantly on '9' or '10', and it had been for as long as I could remember. But still I was dumbstruck. "PTSD?" I queried. "Well, how can I have PTSD? I wasn't in war?" I had always thought you got Post Traumatic Stress Disorder from seeing horrible things or being in terrifying situations in war; from killing, seeing killing, or nearly being killed. I thought it was from watching your buddies get shot, or their legs blown off, or something similar. I have got friends that that has happened to, so I understand why they have PTSD, but I had got out of the military just before the first Gulf War so I didn't see any of that stuff. "Well, it's not always that," Stacy said. "It's likely to be something else traumatic that has happened to you. Something you might have forgotten which is nevertheless still affecting you."

Once Stacy had promised me whatever anti-depressant pills I needed, and she was happy that I was fit to leave, I drove away from the clinic and headed for home, still in a daze. So now I had a diagnosis but no idea how I had come to have PTSD. For the rest of the day my head was in a whirl as I thought back over my life, searching for a clue to the cause of my illness. For sure there were some traumatic events; plenty of things I wished I had never done; people I had hurt when a red rage had gripped me. I cringed at the memory of times I had put people in hospital and damaged myself too. But, really? PTSD? I thought back over my military career for any hint as to when I might have seen or done anything to bring on such a traumatic reaction. And then a terrible secret began to nag at me; a secret that I had tucked as deep into the recesses of my mind as I possibly could, and suddenly I caught a glimpse of the monster that had dogged me my whole adult life. For 35 years I had buried it, determined never to speak about it to a single person; too ashamed to tell my family, my friends, my lovers, anyone. I tried to bury it again then. It couldn't be that, could it? I slept badly that night, tormented by the monstrous secret that now kept rising to the surface of my consciousness and that refused to go away. I struggled all the next day to concentrate on anything, still bothered by the thought that nagged at me but which I was still not ready to confront, let alone to tell anyone else about. It took another sleepless night before I could work up the courage to make a new appointment to see Stacy and the following day I returned to the VA clinic. But where to begin? There were more tears as I tried to find the words to explain the memory that had resurfaced, though at least this time the crying was not uncontrollable. And yet, voicing something I had not told a living soul for 35 years took every ounce of my courage. Stacy listened patiently, gently coaxing information out of me, allowing me to reveal my secret pain in my own time. Something – perhaps God – was compelling me to remember fully and to talk about what had happened so long ago. "There was one thing," I started, and then I had to steel myself to go on. "When I was 19…" I began to explain. I hesitated for a few more seconds before I managed to tell Stacy: "I was in the Army…." The sentence just hung there, unfinished. The words I needed to speak seemed to stick in my throat and I gulped hard to try to dislodge them. "Something happened to me," I blurted out. Stacy looked at me sympathetically, urging me with her eyes to say the unsayable. I bit my lower lip and then, with a quiet voice that seemed to come from the very depths of my soul, I managed to finally utter the words that had been eating away at me for so long. "I … I was raped."

CHAPTER ONE

The perspiration dripping from my forehead stung my eyes and a shimmering heat haze distorted anything more than a few meters away from me, but there was nothing indistinct about the drill sergeant's booming, bullying voice relentlessly shouting at me. The brim of his hat was digging into the side of my head so that his mouth was just an inch or so from my ear and, in spite of the searing temperature, I could feel his breath and the flecks of spittle as he cursed and berated us. "Drop!" he ordered, and I got down as quickly as I could into the push-up position and started pumping. "You're pathetic, you useless maggot! Is that all you've got?" He demanded, though not quite so politely! And not just of me, but of all of us. My arms still screamed from my exertions minutes before on the metal monkey bars, worn shiny by the hands of the thousands of recruits who had swung from them over the decades and turned scalding hot by the unforgiving South Georgia sun. Now the asphalt on the edge of the exercise square burned my already blistered palms as the drill sergeant demanded more push-ups. I was used to warm and dry summers in central Oregon, where I had spent my late teenage years, but the temperature in Fort Benning, 'Home of the US Infantry', was a whole different animal. With 85 degrees heat and 90 per cent humidity the air felt like it was burning my lungs and my body was leaking sweat like a water barrel peppered with buckshot. My army-issue PT shirt stuck to me like I'd been for a swim in it, and steam was imperceptibly rising from all of our bodies as we strained to complete the demanded repetitions. I could sense the eyes watching us from the battalion building overlooking the PT area and just knew they would be enjoying the sight of fresh meat being 'smoked' in 'the pit'.

It was my first week of basic training with my unit and it was brutal. Welcome to Combat Arms. From the moment they shaved your hair off, so you're all the same, they made it clear they regarded us as worthless nobodies, fit only to be broken and then put back together in their image. I had had a vague idea what to expect but waiting in line for my turn, as the razors whirred and the floor filled with the hair of the guys in front of me, was more dehumanizing than I could ever have foreseen and I imagined how sheep must feel at shearing time. Next they overwhelmed us with huge duffle bags stuffed full of gear which they made us empty out, then re-pack, then empty out again, and re-pack again, over and over. And that was before we were introduced to our decrepit World War II barracks. Not that the staff were remotely ready for us to crash exhausted on to our bunks at that stage. Hell, no. They wasted no time in starting the physical torture that would become part of our daily routine. I was in good shape and had never failed any PT exercise before but the heat was killing us and the drill sergeant was not about to make the slightest allowances for it. Unfortunately for me, I'm someone who doesn't know when to quit. I don't understand other people's low pain tolerances. I'm good at ignoring whatever pain I'm in, enjoying 'the suck' as they call it, so when the drill sergeant demanded I keep going, I did. Coming from small-town Oregon, I'd never even talked to a black or brown person in my life. Now I had one screaming in my face. "You are all idiots," he informed me, "and we are here to teach you how to *not* be idiots. Are you listening to me, soldier?" I managed an agonized "Yes, Drill Sergeant," before the heat haze seemed to cloud my vision entirely. My head was pounding, my temples throbbed, and the sunlight seemed to be getting brighter and brighter and brighter until I blacked out and crumpled to the ground. I came round as they threw my limp, over-heated body, still fully clothed, on to the ceramic tiles of the showers and turned on the taps to cool me down. A steady stream of lukewarm water was pouring down on top of me. My head was still pounding and the drill sergeant was still screaming at me. I closed my eyes to see if the pain would go away. He wouldn't.

For a moment, at least, I was a small kid again in Newport, Oregon, the rain coming down in sheets from the silver-grey clouds that swept in from the ocean and pouring in torrents from the roof tiles into over-flowing gutters. It always seemed to rain in Newport. We lived two blocks from the beach but we hardly ever went because it was usually too cold and wet. I think it must have rained nine months of the year and even in summer it never got hot. That didn't stop me from hanging out every day after school with my friends, often until late. Dad worked six days a week as a marine electronics repair man. Mom worked too and my two older sisters weren't usually around either when I might otherwise have gone home. So I didn't, much. Well, not until after it turned dark. I just hung out, riding my bike here, there and everywhere, sometimes getting up to mischief, but it was a small town and my dad was a city commissioner at one point so if I was out causing trouble he pretty quickly knew about it. People called me 'RP' – for Ronald Paul – or sometimes 'Scrawny Ronnie'. It was fair enough. I was tiny as a young boy – super-thin. A stiff breeze could have blown me over, and we had plenty of breeze in Newport, but I didn't bother too much about the wind and the rain and, if allowed, me and my buddies would play outside until the streetlights came on, whatever the weather. I was a real latchkey kid, but that was cool. It was the Seventies and a much more trusting time. Either the door at home was left open or the key would be left in a vehicle for me, unlocked on the street. The doors in our neighbourhood were left unlocked at night too. That was the kind of safe, tiny town it was, filled with middle-class white people, most of whom were either fishermen or loggers, or housewives. Nothing much of note seemed to happen in Newport and it was a big deal when

McDonalds came to town. My school – Sam Case Elementary – was named after some dude who'd been one of the founders of the town, apparently, but even he had done nothing of note, as far as I was aware, apart from fathering a lot of kids.

It was raining as usual one day at school when I was in fourth grade and we were stuck indoors in the cafeteria at recess. I kicked my heels in frustration at not being able to play outside and watched with increasing annoyance as a kid called Johnny bullied some of the other kids. Johnny's dad was a state trooper and he himself was big and chubby and everyone was physically afraid of him and he played on that. He'd tried intimidating me too but I was not susceptible to that crap. Even at that age, I think, I was able to look after myself. I was never one to take a backward step and there was something in me that made me feel it was my job to protect those not able to protect themselves. The longer I watched, the more I grew tired of Johnny picking on everybody until suddenly I'd had enough. He was up on the stage area at that point, throwing his weight around, leaving other kids in tears, and I just walked up to him and punched him, right in front of everybody. With just one shot I put him down and made him cry. Then I walked away. As it happened, Johnny and I became good friends after that but at the time he had just pushed the wrong button with me, and that was a big moment. There were other scraps with other kids after that, but nothing major. It's not like I ran around looking to fight people, but I would go up to any kid I saw bullying and I would say: "Hey! Knock it off or you and I are going to go," and they would usually back off. That incident with Johnny had kind of set the tone and the message had got out: "RP Carter is not to be messed with; that dude will smack you." And I would. I learned early that if I gave the impression that I was dangerous then people would think twice about attacking me. It meant I'd occasionally end up in the principal's office waiting for my dad to pick me up after I'd been involved in some kind of scrap and Dad would look sternly at me as the principal spelled out why I was there, but as soon as we left the building the first question he always asked was: "Did you win?" It makes me cry now to think of it. You shouldn't be asking a boy that. It just taught me violence and competitiveness were OK and I was definitely raised to fight, if necessary, and to win. And it didn't stop my dad taking the belt to me when I got home, for having ended up in the principal's office. Those were the years when my dad would regularly get the belt out if he thought he needed to, and my mom would use a spoon or a piece of kindling if I had stepped out of line. More than once after a punishment I was told to stop crying or I would be given something to cry about but, like I said, it was the Seventies and I wasn't the only kid being told that. I found that hard. I was a reasonably bright kid and I wanted to know why I felt how I felt, and why, if I did something wrong, it was wrong, but it was the era of Baby Boomer parents who weren't great at communication, so we would just be told, 'Shut up,' and, in answer to the question 'Why?', we would be told, 'Because I said so,' or, 'Because I told you to.' We – boys in particular – were brought up to 'man up', to not complain, and to bottle up any feelings. And I'm not sure how much that has changed, sadly. More often than a beating, I would just get grounded, or be given extra chores, but there was a time when Johnny and I were making crank calls, back when the combined local dialling code and a person's house telephone number, together, were only five digits. I think it was the 6th grade and by then Johnny - my former adversary - and I were as thick as thieves. We'd call people to tell them stuff like, "Hey, your refrigerator's running," and when, after a moment's confusion, they agreed that, of course, their refrigerator was running, we'd tell them, "Well you'd better go catch it!" Yes, I know! But it was hilarious to two ten-year-olds. Of course, there was an operator who patched the calls through and could listen in so we got caught pretty quickly and Johnny's cop dad got notified and he told my dad and so we both got into big trouble. I got the belt that time too, but my abiding memories are of a happy childhood, far better than my dad had

had.

His own father had a really tough 'Grapes of Wrath' upbringing, one of 13 children brought up with precious little food in the Oklahoma dust bowl in the mid-to-late 30s. So my grandfather, who came out with his family on the Oregon Trail to build aircraft carriers for the war effort in the 40s, stood no bullshit. One time my dad came home from the Coastguard station where he worked, he told me, and confronted his older brother, who always used to beat him up, and they had started beating hell out of each other and my grandfather got called home from his own work to sort it out and he just smacked the both of them in the face with the butt of a rifle and knocked them both out. So that's how things were in the Grover-Carter household, and it wasn't just his kids that my grandfather was brutal with. I watched him kick my grandmother when he thought she didn't have enough meat on the table when I was visiting. But I also watched my grandmother pop barn kittens in the head with a hammer because my grandfather didn't want an excess of cats but didn't want to do it himself. She once made my father wear a dress as a punishment when he was a boy. What with the strict discipline from his parents and all the beatings he took from his older brother, I guess my dad just wanted to make sure I grew up able to look after myself. I can tell you my father did better by me than his parents did by him so mine might not have been the perfect upbringing but I'm grateful it wasn't his.

Anyway, there I was, running around town, this very active, long-haired, blue-eyed hyper-active boy, always blessed with a lot of athletic ability and a pretty high IQ; lazy from a book-reading point of view - I should have made more of myself, for sure – but I almost always got good grades, mainly because I had to get Bs and above or I didn't get to play sports, and sport is what I lived for. I played every sport I could. I did baseball, I played basketball and I was on the swim team. I think my mother just really wanted to keep me busy because the only way I wouldn't get in everyone's hair was if I was pretty much exhausted at the end of the day. Swimming was great for that and I would swim my little heart out. I loved the water and it exhausted me. My father never really wanted me playing football, but I did a little bit of that too when I was young. Then, later in high school, in defiance of my dad, I would play football again and I would make varsity, chosen for the starting squad of the high school team. In the meantime, I did karate from a young age – not so much for the sport but to make myself – you know, 'Scrawny Ronnie' – someone who you didn't want to pick on. I was ten when I first started karate but that was more than a little strange. My 'teacher' was just a teenager himself but supposedly he was a black belt and my mom hooked me up with him. At my karate lessons he would give me shots of black velvet! At ten years old! Newport was such a weird town, but I guess many small towns are weird like that. Wrestling was another sport I would later get into, as soon as I was at high school. Like the swimming, wrestling is crazy strenuous and it would exhaust me, but, as I said, I enjoy 'the suck' and when something gets really bad is when I get excited and I'm more likely to cry: "Let's go! Let's do this!" than to quit. But that was still in the future as I cycled my way around Newport. Because my father worked six days a week I would spend many Saturdays with him at work. That is, I would play around all day on the Bayfront, by the marine supply store, causing mischief. If I pushed it too far I'd end up grounded or with extra chores, pulling weeds or shovelling manure from the kennels where my parents trained Labradors for bird hunting. On Sundays I would go duck or deer hunting with my father or we would shoot trap, so I got to be really good with a shotgun at an early age. I loved it and it would stand me in good stead later in my Army career.

I was 12 when my parents split up. There were no big fights; no slanging matches, or if there were I don't remember them. Dad was a workaholic so it was not unusual for him not to be around, but I just woke up one day and he was living, temporarily, in some trailer out at the Toledo Trap Club where we used to shoot trap. I didn't learn until later that he had been seeing another woman. Obviously my mom sent me out to hang out with him and he took me for a walk and he told me: "Well, your mom and I aren't getting along so well," and he gave me the old, "We both love you still" line. Things were obviously not great between them but I think they did their best to protect us kids from most of the bullshit. I get it. I don't know if it was right or wrong but I can't go back and change any of it. I don't remember being sad about it all but, nevertheless, it was inevitable that our lives would change, and they did.

CHAPTER TWO

My largely carefree childhood in Newport was coming to an abrupt end and, as happens for so many teenagers, my formative years were about to get a little more complicated. My father ended up marrying Diana, the woman he cheated on my mom with, and my mom moved to Bend, Oregon. She already hated the wind and the rain of Newport, where my father had grown up, and all the stuff that goes along with life in a small town on the Oregon coast. Bend is high desert and it's dry with 300 days a year of sunshine, so she was happier there. Robin, my eldest sister, had already discovered boys and left home by then. My other sister Michelle and I moved with Mom, initially, and I started at Pilot Butte Junior High in Bend but, like any kid would, I struggled a bit. I'd been used to growing up in a small town of maybe 5,000 people where I knew everyone and they knew me. Bend wasn't particularly big, but it had nearly twenty times the population of Newport and it was harder to make friends, so I moved back with my dad who, by then, was in Siletz, Oregon, an even smaller town just ten miles or so inland from Newport, where he and Diana had set up home. At the same time, Michelle moved back to Newport to stay with another family. My stepmom Diana was much younger than my father. She was a writer for Equus Magazine and from a wealthy family that owned cemeteries and she and my father had built this big horse farm on ten acres, with 40 stalls. I don't know what sort of life I thought I would have living with my father but I probably imagined it would be like before, with me and him regularly hunting and shooting together whenever the opportunity arose. It wasn't. Dad was still working six days a week and now running the horse farm as well, so I was shovelling horse shit every day of my life instead of doing sports and fun after-school stuff. Perhaps the only good thing was that it's probably where I learned my strong work ethic, because I had to feed and water all 40 stalls, and muck out 20 of them, every day. On the weekends I was bucking hay, mending fence or doing some other task that had to be done. My relationship with my stepmom was not good and my father did not seem to care. His priority was Diana, first and foremost, and the farm second. I was a distant third, and Diana was certainly no maternal influence. She became the 'step-monster' as far as I was concerned, probably through no fault of her own. I mean, she was in her mid-twenties and had no idea what she was getting into with an older man who had kids and who was pretty much willing to ignore them. There was nothing horrible about her but her interest was the horses. She didn't cook, didn't clean house – had no idea how to - and there were no motherly instincts whatsoever. There I was, a 13-year-old boy, away from his mom, and I needed some feminine energy and I wasn't getting any from her. They wanted me to ride horse, I wanted to ride dirt bikes; they wanted me cleaning out stables, I wanted to play football; in fact, I wanted to play any sport I could. I did ride horses, of course, and I got good at it, but it wasn't my idea of fun. And I certainly didn't want to be shovelling shit constantly. My friends would come over and be like, "How do you stand the smell of this horse shit?" and I was like, "I don't smell it. My nose is blind to it." I could go roll around in the huge mound of horse manure that I had created - and which I would then have to take to the neighbours for their gardens - and I would not smell it. I got decent grades at middle school and quickly made new friends, but being ignored at home sort of prompted me to play up with my stepmom, so that failed social experiment came to an end when I was 15 and my father shipped me off to my mom because I was causing problems in his relationship with Diana. He did have the good grace, years later, to admit that he sent the wrong person away.

So I went back to my mom, in Bend, and by then she was in a relationship with an artist-come-car-salesman and that wasn't much better than I had just left behind. They would hit the wine pretty hard each night and he would get angry when drunk. He beat the hell out of me once, but I threw myself into friendships at my new school, Mountain View High, as a distraction from more bullshit at home. I was back playing sports again and I think that helped me to fit in with my new school friends. I also did pretty well in class. I was a decent student. My school years were challenging, sure, but I remember them fondly because high school was fun. In my senior year my mom left the wino and moved to Portland and she let me stay behind to finish school. I stayed with various friends but Ma and Pa Combs became my surrogate parents. Their daughter Dani was dating my best buddy Gary and we always hung out at the Combs' house so we became very close. I still consider them to be my extended family, and Dani to be my surrogate sister. By then, any childhood dream I had had of being supported in my athletics, or making a career out of sport, had probably already died. I did get a partial scholarship to a small state school – either Eastern Oregon or Southern Oregon University, I think - but without either parent advising me to go to college I decided to join the Army with Gary. If they had pushed me to go to college I probably would have gone and I wouldn't have gone into the Army but that's how it was. I knew they didn't really have the money for me to go to college and even if they could scrape it together I would probably just party through college and get kicked out and wind up in some blue-collar job on the Oregon coast, in oil or logging or fishing, or just working my ass off, and I didn't really want that. When it came to the Armed Service Vocational Aptitude Battery (ASVAB) – the military entrance tests - I did well – in the top 5% in the country - and could have joined any branch of the services and done pretty much any job I wanted, but my buddy was not a stellar student. We later learned Gary had dyscalculia – he was dyslexic with numbers – and he pretty much got through high school by cheating off me at math. I thought I was being a good friend at the time by letting him but maybe if I hadn't he would have got the help he needed sooner. Anyway, Gary's low score on the entrance tests meant he could only join the infantry – Combat Arms. That was fine with him. I think he would have joined the infantry whatever and he was my buddy so I joined with him and the Army said they would keep us together, which was important to us. I kind of felt like a protector to Gary, but he was kind of a protector to me too. My teachers reckoned I was smart and should hold out for officer training but, like I said, without any counselling from either parent to go to college or push for a better military career, I was happy to go with Gary and the recruiters were just happy to get us in to Combat Arms. I told my parents, "Well, I'm joining the Army and they'll pay for my schooling later." We both joined on a delayed entry program so that we could put off recruit training for a year and complete high school but I let my school grades go. I basically stopped putting the effort in and instead of getting Bs and As, which I was capable of, I got a D, a couple of Cs, and some Bs and As in stuff that was super easy. I stayed on really because I wanted to continue with my sports. Oh, and because, like so many other boys at that age, I had discovered sex. By then I had a steady girlfriend and she was the love of my life.

At that age my machismo was raging but it was much more than that. It felt grown up to have a steady girlfriend and to be having sex, and there was a softness and vulnerability to my sweetheart that really appealed to the protector in me. She was the perfect balance to the coarseness of my male friendships and while I felt like a knight in shining armour, the oxytocin rushing through my veins knocked the rough edges off the soaring levels of testosterone. When she fell pregnant, I didn't freak out about it as I suppose I should have done. I was 17 and certainly immature, which was probably why I didn't foresee the enormous problems that would come with our situation and why I so readily accepted that I would just have to step up to be a father. In my head I was a pretty stand-up guy, who took his responsibilities seriously and I was looking at it through rose-tinted glasses. I wanted to marry my sweetheart; my first true love. I envisaged us bringing up our child in Army family accommodation, and being less laissez-faire parents than my own mom and dad had been. But my girlfriend's father had other ideas. He already thought I was a dead loss because I was joining the infantry and that I was not good enough for his princess, which was a bit rich. He and his wife might have been wealthy but they were by no means the perfect parents themselves, I would later learn. Anyway, pretty quickly after my sweetheart found she was pregnant her dad told her in no uncertain terms she would not be keeping the child and that he would be making an appointment for her at a clinic in North Dakota. A few weeks later I came of age but there was no big party, probably just a few illicit beers with my mates. My dad was not there, my mom was not there and, as it happened, my sweetheart was not there either. Her father had squirreled her off to North Dakota, as promised, to abort our baby - on my 18th birthday, which was pretty horrific. I'm all about a woman having the choice over her body but it would have been humane to at least have informed me, if not to have discussed it with me and to give me a say about our child. I'll never forget that feeling of hurt for as long as I live. Not that my sweetheart was given much of a choice either. In spite of my upset over the abortion, my sweetheart and I decided to stay together as a couple but my delayed entry period was coming to an end. On July 22, 1986, having sworn my love for my girl, I left for Georgia and the start of basic training and she then went off to San Diego State University.

July in Georgia was scorching. It took a day to in-process us to our unit Delta 9/2 and to our old wooden World War Two barracks at Harmony Church, Fort Benning. 'The Church' has since been torn down but veterans of that place knew it as 'Agony Church'. It was regarded by many as the toughest training for infantrymen anywhere on earth at the time. The US Army had been training infantrymen at Fort Benning since 1918 and Harmony Church barracks felt like it had been there all that time. They were that old. Each building housed around 40 of us in open dormitories, on old steel bunk beds, with no air conditioning and just old fans at the end of each row of bunks to help offset the stifling heat and humidity. Fights would often break out over who got the fan closest to them. The only things thriving in those conditions were the cockroaches. I'd never seen one before I arrived in Georgia but now they were my regular bed mates. More than once I awoke in the night with a cockroach on my sweaty chest. The bathrooms had no stalls, just open toilet pans and two sinks, and the shower area had just three shower heads. It was impossible to keep the barracks clean to the satisfaction of the drill instructors and they took full advantage. They knew that if we had just cleaned our room they only had to bang on the walls and the dust of decades would cover it again, so when it was inspection time that's exactly what the instructors would do, then they would demand that we make a better job of cleaning. We used to look longingly at the Sand Hill barracks nearby, which were newly-built from concrete and had air-conditioning. We knew them as the 'Sand Hilton' and the instructors rubbed it in our faces often, but claimed we would be all the tougher for having come through Harmony Church rather than softer options. The physical training pit was large and filled with sawdust and if the heat and the exertion didn't break you, the fire ants just might. A couple of the soldiers in our intake were attacked by them and had to go to hospital. They were lucky to survive, we were told. There was no indoor training option. If we weren't in the training pit we would be running around dirt roads on the base, whatever the weather, but that was cool with me because I was a pretty good runner. Other aspects of life in barracks were not so familiar. Having been brought up in small town Oregon, and never previously seen anyone of colour, the drill sergeants were not the only black faces now in my life. Around half of our platoon was non-white, but I was never raised to hate and so I was happy to be part of this diverse new group and we all got along pretty well. It would be a while before the military decided if we were going to be ground-pounders, mortar men, tow-missile crewmen or Bradley drivers, or whatever. To start with we were just learning infantry basics and that meant dismantling everything we thought we had ever known, like how to walk, how to look, how to stand, how to hold your shoulders, neck, back and stomach, and retraining us on how it should be done. They taught us the only answers we were ever allowed to use in response to a senior rank, and even the tone we could give the answers in. As a boy who grew up hating that I never got a proper answer to the question 'Why?' I now had to come to terms with the fact that I could never even ask 'Why?' but just do. Often that meant being forced to do the dumbest crap, over and over. They would make us paint rocks, just to bring us down, and other meaningless tasks so that you would learn to take orders without question; to be prepared to charge up that hill not caring that there was a machine-gun waiting. And it worked. When they said, "Jump!" we asked, "How high? Sir!" Because I showed a propensity for helping other recruits they paired me up with a fat oaf from Oregon who was big and not very bright and who struggled to even button his shirt correctly. But, you know, the likes of a senator's son is never going to get recruited into Combat Arms. It is unfortunately the poor and uneducated, who have experienced trauma and who have other priorities ahead of academic classes, who usually end up in Combat Arms. The military promises you schooling and a pay check and three square meals a day and to make you into a man and that is generally attractive to those from less privileged backgrounds.

There were a few issues between us recruits, and a few scraps here and there, but not too many. Usually you would call someone out to settle a score beyond the wood line, away from the barracks, and go to it. We were, after all, young and poor and that is how things got settled. Just a few black eyes and fat lips. No one was trying to kill each other. We were just establishing a pecking order of dominance. We were brothers in arms and, regardless of colour, we were going to fight together and likely die together so we became a team and cared enough about each other to go to war together. To be honest, I didn't mind the hardships, and the tough training, but there was one occasion when I blew my top. We came back to our barracks and it had been 'tossed' by the instructors, with all of our things scattered around the bunks, which was not unusual, but I had a picture of my sweetheart and it had fallen into a bucket of mop water, and I completely lost it. I stormed in to see Drill Sergeant Green and started screaming and shouting and telling him that I had had enough and that I was out of there. The drill sergeant was pretty smart and could see I was upset so he heard me out then told me that he was happy to let me go but on condition that I first took an 8lb sledgehammer and went to break up a nearby strip of concrete sidewalk that was being turned into rubble. Of course, after I had pummelled the concrete for a good while I had calmed down, so I went back to see the sergeant to tell him that I didn't want to leave after all. Besides, because of my high test scores I often got selected for some fun tasks now and then, and the long runs that some guys struggled with were easy for me. They used to have a fast group and a slow group, and me and my buddy Gary quickly got chosen for the fast group led by Drill Sergeant Haylock, who was a marathon runner. I would run right on the heels of Sergeant Haylock and give him grief. "Hey, old man, you can't bring smoke! Pick it up old man, let's go. I'm not even breathing hard yet. Why are you breathing so hard?" What was nice was that when we were really exercising hard like that, he would put up with my insolence because he knew I was just playing. And he knew that I could outrun him.

After the first weeks of basic training we went to advanced individual training to hone our individual killing skills. We lucked out after that when we got a slot at airborne school so Gary and I stayed on at Fort Benning and learned how to jump out of airplanes. That was a blast and we got our weekends off for the first time in many months. I flew to California to look up my dad who was down there and I visited my sweetheart at San Diego State. It was so good to see her, but I couldn't help but think that something felt different. I put the slight awkwardness down to her being surrounded by her new college friends who were very different to my army buddies, but we looked forward to catching up properly when we were both back in Bend next. I threw myself into the last stages of training and finally I got home on leave a couple of weeks before Christmas, visiting family and my girlfriend. It was so good to see her, not just because I had missed her smile and her softness but because my hormones were raging more than ever after so long away without her. We soon made up for the time we had spent apart and the sex was amazing. I told her all about life at Fort Benning and she told me more about University and the two worlds could not have been more different. With her in my arms it didn't matter but, in what seemed like a matter of days, my leave was over. Gary and I learned that our next posting would be in Germany. It felt like a big move, a long way from home, but we had each other to lean on and I promised I would write regularly to my parents and to my sweetheart. Nevertheless it felt gut-wrenching as I once again professed my undying love to her and we said our sad goodbyes. So this was it. I was ready for the first really big adventure in my life.

CHAPTER THREE

The blonde flight attendant looked immaculate in her tailored skirt, waistcoat, jacket and yellow scarf as she leaned over the trolley towards Gary and me and, with a beautiful smile, asked: "Would you gentlemen like anything from the bar? A beer perhaps?" For two 18-year-olds from Oregon, the Lufthansa flight from San Francisco to Frankfurt, Germany, was like nothing we had ever experienced before. For a start, the drinking age in the US was 21. Would we like a beer? Hell, yeah we would! After months of being treated as worthless punks at basic training, this was a level of sophistication we were going to make the most of for the next few hours at least. After that, who knew? But my buddy and I would face the future together, whatever our new posting held in store for us. The Army had only told us: "You're going to Germany. This is the flight to book yourselves on. Call these people when you land and we'll come and get you." That was it, so we settled into our seats, too excited to sleep, and looked out of the windows in awe as we flew over Canada, Greenland, Iceland, and miles upon miles of open ocean. We were world travellers now and we flashed the stewardess the broadest grins every time she passed our seats with that beer-laden trolley.

It's not that we got smashed or anything, but my memory of flying into Frankfurt is fuzzy. We just made our way through the airport, through baggage collection and passport control, and emerged into the arrivals hall, found a phone and put in a call to the number we had been given. Then we waited until we spotted the guy holding up a board with our names on it. That was the start of 'in-processing' and that's when the first hammer blow struck. We were being separated, we discovered, and Gary was being sent to 'K-Town' – Kaiserslautern. So much for the recruiting sergeant's promise that we would be able to stay together! In the blink of an eye Gary was gone and I suddenly felt very alone as I was whisked off somewhere completely different. I could not even tell you if there were other guys in the transport sent to collect me from the airport. My mind was a blur. I only recall that I ended up in a vast hall laid out with bunk beds for around 40 people. Where the hell I was, or who the hell the other guys were I had no idea. I just remember that the hall was very dimly lit. Maybe that was typical of post-war Germany at that time, far less modernised than I was used to in the US, or maybe the darkness is etched into my brain because my abiding memory is of lying on my bunk, my bottom lip trembling, trying to talk myself out of crying when 'lights out' was announced. I don't remember being shown the slightest kindness or warmth in that place. I was 18, on my own, surrounded by strangers, and it was mid-December so it was bitterly cold. Look, those are never going to be the cheeriest of places. No one is going to offer you a nice warm cocoa and a place by the fire while you acclimatise to your surroundings, and I had been in Fort Benning, so I had kind of got off the teat a little bit there, but for a young boy, 5,000 miles from home for the first time in his life, it was scary and I silently cried myself to sleep.

The next morning I was moved to the US Army garrison at Bamberg, where my new unit - the First (Battalion) of the 52nd infantry - was based. The 52nd was a mechanised infantry regiment that had a pretty good World War Two history but the Warner Barracks – built in 1936 for the German Wehrmacht but occupied by US Infantry from April 1945 - were as gloomy as the hall I had spent my first night in Germany in: red brick admin buildings linked by cobbled roads to rows of classic Bavarian-style four-storey accommodation blocks that had somehow escaped being bombed in the war or knocked down after it. At least at Bamberg we had rooms, rather than all being in one giant space as I had been at Fort Benning. The non-commissioned officers (NCOs) who did not live off-post had their own rooms, typically smaller than ours but they had them to themselves. Any enlisted men like me – E4 rank (Specialist) down to E2 (Private) – got thrown in together, four to a room, with a locker each, and all of your stuff had to be squared away in there, neat and tidy. You had to have your Class A's (formal uniform) in there and your BDUs (camouflaged battle dress uniform) and they all had to be ironed and hung up. Your duffle bag went on top and all your extra gear went in the locker, in an orderly fashion and ready to go at a moment's notice. It was pretty intimate in that small room, so the four of us were going to have to get along, but not before some pecking orders had been established. It wasn't long before I got into a fight with one of my first room-mates – a black kid from The Bronx, New York. I had grown up in a small rural town, hunting most weekends, so he probably considered me to be a hillbilly, and I certainly thought he was a brash city kid. He was only little, like me, but Jesus was he strong. We both were. He probably wrestled in school like me. Anyway, words were said and we smacked each other around a bit and then we were buddies. It was like that with most of the unit. We were all in it together so we might as well get used to it. I hadn't been in the barracks for more than a few days before a couple of guys who had been there a while offered to introduce me to the delights of Bamberg, and took me out drinking on the Friday night. Now, in America at the time, even those who were legally old enough to drink drank piss-water weak beer so my introduction to some real strong European alcohol was always going to go badly. We started off drinking German beer in an Irish bar run by a Turkish couple, just across the street from the base, but where we ended up I couldn't tell you. I can picture the faces of some of the guys but I don't remember their names. What I do remember is that I was badly hungover the next day.

Early training was an introduction for us newbies to the

armoured personnel carriers that would carry us into battle in the event of the brown stuff hitting the fan. I say 'armoured'. The fully tracked, 12 tonnes M113 was made from aluminium alloy so would probably stop small arms fire but an enemy tank could blow it to death, and it seemed to me that a 50 cal would probably pierce it, which is why they were known by all of us as 'fireboxes'. They could hold up to 15 passengers but typically would carry a squad of seven to nine people with a driver, and the NCO manning the 50-caliber, belt-fed, air-cooled M2 Browning machine gun in the turret on top, and that was pretty much our only defence because it didn't matter what weaponry you were carrying, you couldn't do anything with it - like fire at an enemy outside - while you were being transported inside. In those early days, the guys like those who had taken me drinking would take advantage of the naivety of us young newbies at every opportunity. We would be out in the field and one of the more long-term guys would tell one of us: "I think the shocks are broken on the firebox. Go over there and jump up and down on it a bit and let me see what's going on with it." Well, you'd be jumping up and down on what was basically a small tank so it's certainly not going to move the shock-absorbers! You just looked like a jackass. Or they would ask one of us to go to stores to get a can of brake squelch to make the radio sound better, or a box of grid squares for the maps. It was harmless fun and I fell for it. We all did at one time or another. And we would doubtless try it for ourselves on the next lot of newbies to arrive, but for now we were the ones very much wet behind the ears, easy prey for the pranksters, and with every humiliation my home felt like another million miles away. I had an MCI card to make phone calls but, as a private, I was not making a lot of money so I couldn't afford to use it often. My girlfriend, being at college, was living in dorms so, in the days long before cell-phones, I had little chance of talking to her, and when I rang my mom I didn't have the heart to tell her how unhappy I was. I just put on my best macho persona, tried to cough away the tremble in my voice and told her everything was fine.

I had only been there a week or so before Christmas was upon us but there was little festive spirit in evidence and certainly none to spare for me. Bamberg was one of Germany's most beautiful towns, briefly the centre of the Holy Roman Empire and the burial place of Emperor Henry II. For most of the year it was picture postcard pretty with medieval streets and buildings dating from the 11th to the 19th Century nestled beside the Regnitz river including the Romanesque Bamberg Cathedral where Pope Clement II is laid to rest, and the historic town hall on an island in the middle of the Regnitz, reached by cobblestone arched bridges. With snow on the ground, the town was especially picturesque when it was lit up at Christmas time. Warner Barracks, however, were as stark and as unwelcoming as ever and, as the new guy, I was put on all-night duty on Christmas Eve on the Battalion Charge of Quarters (CQ) desk with orders to stay ready to alert the soldiers in the barracks to any emergency orders. It was just me and an NCO. I have no idea who he was and I didn't see him after the first few moments of our night shift when he told me: "I'll be in my room. If there is an emergency come and alert me. Otherwise, just stay up, stay alert and don't fall asleep or you'll be kicked out of the Army so fast your feet won't touch the ground. Understood?" I guess he got a good night's sleep. I certainly didn't. It was the first Christmas I had ever had to work, let alone on my own, so there were tears running down my face and dripping on to the tissue-thin airmail paper as I sat there and wrote letters, one to my mom and one to my girlfriend, telling them how much it sucked to be on all-night duty on Christmas Eve and how lonely I was, an 18-year-old boy spending his first ever Christmas away from family and friends, a very long way from home. My all-night duty ended in the morning and I went back to my room, exhausted, and slept through Christmas Day.

With the festive season out of the way, things started to look up as I threw myself into our daily routines and got to know the rest of the guys in my squad better and learned more about the guys in the three other squads of second platoon, as well as some of those in the three other platoons in our company. We would typically roll out at about 6am or earlier because, as a platoon, we would always have to do PT before breakfast and morning Formation. Every once in a while the commanding officer (CO) would want to have a full company outing, with all four platoons, and that's when my running prowess stood me in good stead. At the end of basic training I weighed 155lbs, I had a 33 inch waist and I could sprint for two miles. In fact, my last two-mile run of basic training - which we all had to do within 15 minutes and 54 seconds in order to pass – I ran in 10 minutes and 34 seconds. I know, compared to the marathon runners of today, that's not something amazing but for a fairly short-legged, five foot nine and half inches white kid, that was moving and I was the number one guy in basic training, so when it came to those company runs in Bamberg I was in my element. If some of the guys were lagging behind at half way then the CO, knowing that I was quick, would get me to run ahead to the chow hall to tell them to stay open because we were out doing PT and would want breakfast when we got back. It was a good feeling to be recognised by the CO and favoured with that responsibility. After a shower we would eat and then fall in for Formation at around 8.30am or 9am. You had to be in your BDUs and they had to look decent enough to pass inspection, but pretty soon I was feeling comfortable enough with most of the NCOs that we could enjoy some banter. Staff Sergeant Dejulio would tell me on a regular basis: "Private Carter, you lie, your feet stink and you don't love Jesus!" It was just this funny thing he liked to say to me as a joke because I don't lie, my feet don't stink and I do love Jesus. After Formation we would train in our squads and our platoon, familiarising ourselves with our 'Firebox' or practising our soldiering skills and we'd try to be done by 5pm Retreat, an after any end of day formation, unless we were out in the field on an exercise. Then the rest of the evening was our own.

Being January, it was already dark before we finished work one particular day. After a meal in the chow hall I headed back to my room and lay down on my bunk with a letter I had been handed that morning from the latest mail delivery. It took weeks to get letters back and forth and any communication from home was so precious that I had been looking forward to this moment all day. With some trepidation I eased open the envelope and I smiled to myself when I saw it was from Dani. I missed my friend. Obviously not as much as Gary would be missing her, but it felt good to hear from her and I looked forward to news from home. My excitement quickly evaporated as the contents of the letter hit me. Dani had been to visit at San Diego State, she wrote, and felt a duty to warn me that my sweetheart was proving to be very popular with the boys of the football team, among others, and was clearly having a very good time without too much concern that she had a boyfriend in Germany. I was overcome with a desperate feeling of emptiness and all I could do was hope against hope that Dani was just being over-protective and that it was not true.

CHAPTER FOUR

My "Dear John" letter arrived soon after. Everyone cries when they get that letter, and everyone deployed overseas gets one. As a young guy, in love with your first girlfriend, you think that you are going to go home and marry her and all the old war movies support that thought. You're going to come home the hero and marry your sweetheart and have kids and the idyllic house and the white picket fence and the whole nine yards, but the reality is a real kick in the guts. The fact is, you're away from home and she has moved on. I cried myself to sleep that night and there was no hiding it from my room-mates and others so I told them the next day. There were a couple of nice guys who asked, 'You alright?' but most of them were like, 'Oh! You got yours did you?' It's such a common occurrence that everybody jokes about it. As young men do, you try to macho it out and try to laugh about it, but all the while you're dying on the inside. It was horrible. I thought back to the time I visited her at college and I remembered thinking then that something was off, but I couldn't put my finger on it. I guess after Dani's visit she thought, 'I've got to let him know. I can't keep stringing this poor bastard along,' and, credit to her, she did. She wrote the letter as nicely as she could but there was no painless way to be told, 'Hey, I'm in college and you're over there and this isn't going to work, so...' It makes it worse that you're already lonely, surrounded by a bunch of dudes - because there were no women in the infantry - and you know the German women, understandably, don't want anything to do with you, so you realise pretty quickly, 'I'm going to be single for the rest of my time here.'

Of course, life had to go on and it did, which meant the usual daily routine, plus regular surprise exercises that we would have sprung on us in the middle of the night. Back then, the Cold War was still very much a thing and we were there in Germany guarding the Iron curtain or, specifically in our case at the time, the fence with Czechoslovakia. We needed to be ready at a moment's notice should the Russian tanks come rolling through so the army chiefs would regularly sound the alert at two, three or four o'clock in the morning and you had to grab your gear and go to your personal M113 ready for action. They certainly did not tell us where we were going, whether it was for real or a drill, or anything like that, which kind of made sense. I mean, if you are going to go to war then you can't afford to be mamby-pamby about it. We were being trained to kill and the alerts happened a lot. When we were not doing routine training, or being woken without warning at some unearthly hour, we would either go for live-fire training at Grafenwoehr, or for more tactical training at Hohenfels. At Hohenfels we would do a lot of work with the 'MILES' – Multiple Integrated Laser Engagement System – which meant we would wear electronic gear which allowed us to fire lasers and 'kill' each other. Grafenwoehr, on the other hand, was a huge range where we could use live ammo, live tanks, live grenades and live M47 'Dragon' missile systems. It was really serious and there was a distinct potential for friendly fire and people getting killed, so you needed to be on your game. When you're talking about guys who aren't always the brightest and you're putting into their hands a light machine gun that fires 850 rounds a minute, that's a dangerous combination. Before the military converted to the M249 SAW while I was in Germany they used the M60 machine gun and I quickly became a '60' gunner. There's an unwritten creed among juniors in the military that you don't stand out if you can help it. Do your best, of course, but excel at your peril because with excellence comes attention – a spotlight – and it is not always welcome attention. Perhaps I didn't get the memo but I wasn't deliberately trying to stand out. I was just doing what came naturally. As mentioned, I grew up shooting professional trap and hunting regularly. I mean, we had 50 weapons in the house all the time so I was very familiar with them. A lot of people who didn't grow up with access to weapons like that were afraid of them and the bangs scared them. I get it, but I had done it thousands and thousands of times. My dad and I would go through a thousand rounds of 12-gauge ammo in a weekend when I was a kid so I was really used to it. Shooting trap gave me a head-start with weapons and I was already proficient with an M16 before joining the army. I had never been afraid of weapons and I was pretty accurate with them. I even think it helped me in my ability to fight because I would keep my eyes open and know what was coming at me, focussing on what I needed to deliver, rather than closing my eyes when a weapon was fired or a missile exploded near me. They also had me be the radio guy at one point, and they gave me stuff like that, not just because of my proficiency with weapons but because I was fit and I could carry it all. The M60, for example, was 23lbs and then you've got your 80lbs ruck sack so that stuff pretty soon gets real heavy and not all the guys could handle it.

By the time I turned 19 in March I had been promoted to Private First Class (E3) and I was growing into my role. And I wasn't the only one. There was another E3 guy - I'll call him Johnson - and he was in a different platoon. He was good looking, very physically fit and definitely the fastest sprinter. I remember trying to outrun the guy a couple of times because I fancied myself as pretty quick but he could run you down in a millisecond. I mean, he was fast. Johnson could not only sprint but he could do push-ups all day, so that bred a certain amount of confidence, which I guess annoyed his platoon NCO who I'll call Staff Sergeant Brown for now. Mind you, it wasn't just Johnson he didn't like, or me. I don't think Staff Sergeant Brown liked anybody. He was just an angry, bitter old bastard. I think he was probably in his mid-thirties, which seemed very old to a 19-year-old like me. He had definitely been in the military for a while and he was still only an E6 rank because he was such a grumpy piece of work. I think he had a pretty low IQ and I imagine that he came from a really, really difficult background. That's pure speculation on my part but you could just feel the anger he had for the world and particularly anyone he felt was superior or had had an easier life than him, or who was better looking than him, which was most people. I could sense when we did full company training - with all the platoons - that he was trying to compete with me, whether it was running or push-ups or anything else, and I would smoke his old arse and I know that it just pissed him off. He was a person who wanted to be able to dominate other people, or at least scare them. He was a bully and I wasn't about to kowtow to him because that's just not in me, but it still baffled me why he seemed to hate me so much. I was just trying to do the best I could and the physical stuff and the soldiering came naturally to me, which I thought should be seen as a good thing by those who were meant to have responsibility for us, like Staff Sergeant Brown. I was blessed with natural fitness and a reasonably high IQ and I wanted to use what I was given for the good of others; I was also full of enthusiasm and I was a sociable kind of person who was always trying to make friends and help other people. So why did Staff Sergeant Brown dislike me so much? I didn't get it. I never spoke to him about it but I could tell the guy just did not like me and it seemed to be from pretty early on.

It was one Friday morning just after Formation broke and some of us guys were milling around waiting to start the day's routines when Staff Sergeant Brown wandered by with a corporal-level soldier (E4) – I'll call him Specialist Morris – and Brown was like, 'Hey, we're having a couple of beers at my place tomorrow. You guys are coming.' And that was pretty much it. It wasn't like any kind of grand gesture, or instruction to the whole group – just to Johnson and me - and I thought, 'That's really weird,' because I did think that he couldn't stand me, and NCOs were not meant to fraternise with enlisted ranks, though it was not strictly enforced. I kept thinking about it over my evening meal and there was definitely a feeling that something was not right but I couldn't decide what it was and there wasn't really anyone I could discuss it with. I may have had a brief conversation with Johnson to decide what time we might meet to share a cab, but we certainly didn't share any misgivings. I don't even know if he was as perplexed by it as I was. It wasn't like I spent much time with him, other than when we were on the same full company exercise, or at Formation, and I wouldn't usually have been with him at meal time in the chow hall. Nor was there anyone I would have mentioned it to among my roommates or drinking buddies, because I don't recall any of them receiving the kind of animosity that I did from Staff Sergeant Brown so it would not seem such an odd instruction to them. I think I gathered that Specialist Morris would be at Brown's place too but it wasn't clear who else would be. The more I thought about it, the more I couldn't shake the sense that something was not quite right but my passion for winning friends overrode any sense of danger and I was just a naïve 19-year-old, thousands of miles from home. I think I just reassured myself that it was an opportunity to show Staff Sergeant Brown that I wasn't a bad person or anyone that he should hate. Maybe over a beer and a barbeque he would chill out a bit and not be forever trying to bully me and maybe I could understand where he was coming from. Besides, Brown was a superior and I felt I couldn't refuse the instruction, even if I had wanted to. I had been raised, and trained, remember, to follow orders not question them.

CHAPTER FIVE

Johnson and I must have met up outside the barracks to get a cab to Brown's place, which was off-post, but it was a fairly short journey across town with not too much conversation before we reached his home in one of the less attractive parts of Bamberg. We paid the cabbie and climbed the steps from the sidewalk to what I guess was the first floor. The city had some really beautiful old buildings but I don't remember Brown's place being one of them, just an ugly, typically pre-war German brick apartment block, which was probably the basic off-post rental accommodation that the US military was prepared to pay for to house a none-too-stellar married NCO with no children. The two of us standing there, waiting for the doorbell to be answered, only felt stranger now that we were actually there. After a short while, Brown opened the door and ushered us into a small, equally dull, dark wood-panelled living room that was lit with fairly low-watt lamps, adding to the ominous feel of the place. Specialist Morris was already there, standing in the living room, but my first surprise was that no-one else was. Particularly noticeable by her absence was Staff Sergeant Brown's wife. Now, I'm from the kind of small community where if you get invited round for a barbeque you get welcomed by the host, thanked for coming, introduced to his wife and other guests and told 'The pig's on the grill, grab yourself a beer and make yourself comfortable'. There was nothing remotely welcoming about Brown's place, or Brown. The atmosphere was chillier than the spring air outside and I sure as hell wasn't promised any food. Nothing felt right, though the stilted attempts at small talk was not a big surprise. Brown was always a pretty obtuse, weird dude so the moments of silence, however uncomfortable, did not seem out of character in the slightest. And yet he was the one who had invited us – no, instructed us – to come for drinks. I put the coolness down to the fact of our different ranks and because we had never before been together in any kind of social setting, only during training, but maybe it was because, unlike Johnson and me, Staff Sergeant Brown and Specialist Morris knew exactly what was about to happen. No sooner had we been told to take a seat on the rather dated furniture than Brown asked if we wanted a beer. Morris, I think, already had one, and when we both said 'Yes' Brown went off to the kitchen, out of sight. Morris, still standing, broke the silence by asking some crap about the previous day's training but he didn't pretend to be very interested in whatever answer we gave, then he shut up again when Brown returned and handed a glass of beer each to Johnson and me. Did I wonder why we had glasses and Brown and Morris were nursing bottles of beer? Was I slightly suspicious when he went out of sight to pour them? I don't know, but I took a couple of decent pulls of my drink to compensate for the awkwardness of the situation as we made a few more half-hearted attempts at chit-chat. If anyone else was coming I hoped they would show up soon pretty damn soon and that I would know them, but no one did and it wasn't long – no more than a minute or two, I think – before I started to feel really weird – hot and nauseous. I presume Johnson did too. The signs of our discomfort must have been obvious and though I couldn't have known it, seeing us both groggy was probably the signal for Brown and Morris to make their move.

Without warning, Morris launched himself across the room towards me. I had no clue why but in spite of my nausea I saw his move clearly and I felt a sudden horrible moment of panic as I realised I was about to be attacked. I immediately tried to stand to defend myself. 'Oh my God!' I thought, 'I'm going to have to fight my way out of here!' But my legs didn't feel like my own and as soon as I realised my limbs did not seem to do what my brain wanted them to, my alarm turned to terror. Even as I prepared to fight, and Morris landed the first few blows to my head, I realised that the lights were going out; that I was falling unconscious. I felt Morris's fists crash into my face, bone on bone, crushing the thin flesh in between with an animal ferocity, and in that awful moment I knew that I was no longer capable of defending myself and I was convinced I was about to be killed. It was terrifying. And then everything went black.

I have no idea how long I was unconscious, or how I was moved from that gloomy living room, but I came to, still hazy, sitting naked on a linoleum floor in what had to be a bathroom because there was a bathtub on one side of the room and a toilet and a basin against another wall. My head pounded. 'Where was I now? And what the hell had happened to my clothes?' I had no idea what time it was or how long I had been in that state. Through the confusing brain fog, I could see Johnson was also naked, sitting in the tub. 'Why?' 'What's going on?' It made no sense at all. And then Brown was lifting me roughly to my feet and trying to make me put my cock in Johnson's mouth. Johnson was slumped against the side of the bathtub nearest to me and looked in no state to do anything about it. I can't remember if Morris was holding Johnson's head to stop it lolling but for a moment I was conscious enough to know that this was all wrong and when I tried to resist it earned me another vicious beating from Brown. Then everything went black again.

How I got back to the barracks, and whether Johnson was with me for the journey, I couldn't tell you. I presume that Brown and Morris would have stuffed us both, still heavily drugged, in a cab and told the cabbie we were drunk and given him instructions where to deliver us. I have a nagging memory that Brown's last malevolent words to me as he led me from his apartment were a warning that if I ever breathed a word of what had taken place he would kill me. I doubt whether the driver, even seeing the state of me, would have paid too much attention. The cabbies were used to picking up drunken GIs and letting them off at the gate to the barracks. The gate guards would just check their ID and send them on their way to their accommodation. If they had marks on their faces - the odd black eye or split lip - then that wasn't super uncommon because GIs would often go out, get drunk and fight each other. I know because I worked the gate from time to time. You just checked their IDs and let them go in because typically you didn't want to create a bunch of paperwork for yourself. If they were crap-faced then you let them go to bed and sleep it off. But I wasn't drunk. Out of it, certainly, but not drunk. I have no recollection of going through the gate or getting back to my room. I'm sure that my face can't have been too mangled otherwise the gate guards might have paid a bit more attention, but it was the damage that they wouldn't have been able to see that was far worse. The exact details of the sexual assault I had suffered I may never know, but the confident 19-year-old Ron Carter with a bright future died that night and what was born into the world was a shabby shadow of my former self.

CHAPTER SIX

I woke in the half-light with a thumping headache, a wave of nausea and an overwhelming feeling of confusion. With an effort, I turned to look at the clock on the wall and felt bruised and aching all over. At least I was in my own bed and my roommates were not stirring so I reckoned it must be early Sunday morning but my memories of the day before were still a blur. I eased myself awkwardly out of bed and pain shot through my body as I struggled to stand. With difficulty I got myself upright and moved as quietly as I could to the bathroom to avoid disturbing my room mates but worse discomfort was slowly penetrating my fogged brain and sparking alarming flashes of memory. 'What the hell had happened to me?' I reached the bathroom, shut the door behind me and lowered my shorts. My cock hurt when I peed and I had an injury to my rectum that was now burning with a searing pain, like red-hot shards of metal being shoved up inside of me. I manoeuvred uncomfortably, anxious not to exacerbate the pain, and tried to examine myself in the bathroom mirror. Even with an incomplete view I could see my butt was messed up. There was blood and clear signs of injury and though I wasn't sure how, or by whom, I realized with horror that I had been raped. I tried desperately to piece together a few disjointed memories from the previous day in an effort to answer the avalanche of questions going through my aching head. That was the worst feeling – the not knowing and not being able to fill in the traumatic voids. The image of sitting in Brown's living room did become clear and the moment of horror when I had come under attack and feared I would be killed as I was falling unconscious was all too vivid and I mentally recoiled from it. The brief memory of that bathroom and the disgusting pastel shades – like some pre-war building that had been modernised in the early Seventies and never updated since – also danced in my vision and I shuddered when I remembered being naked and beaten, but any further details remained agonisingly out of reach of my recall. I moved again and another jolt shot through my rectum like a burning flame. I grimaced. I could take the pain. I was used to pushing through physical hurt. I took bodily discomfort as a challenge to push myself harder, but the worst injury was to my pride. The knowledge that I had been defiled was like a dagger to my soul, shattering my self-esteem, and leaving my teenage sense of invincibility torn to shreds. I felt dirty and worthless. Who had done what to me I couldn't know exactly, and nor was I about to tell anyone what little I did know. I had been out on drunken nights before and I had got into fights and you just didn't nark; you didn't tell. But this was a whole different level of secrecy. I had this injury to my ass and, being a young macho kid, full of masculine ego, I sure as hell wasn't going to tell anyone about that. I would rather die. And then the ramifications of what had happened began to dawn on me and I broke into a cold sweat. 'What if they accuse me of being gay?' I could be dishonourably discharged from the army, because that's what happened if you were gay in the army back then. Apart from the disgrace, a dishonourable discharge would mean I would lose the right to all sorts of school, health or financial benefits if I needed them in future. I'd be finished, I was sure, and I'd be lucky not to end up in jail because that's what I thought could happen. The rumours were that the military prison they would send you to at Fort Leavenworth was far tougher than ordinary jails, so, as a 19-year-old boy, I was seriously scared. I had grown up around gay people and had no problem with them. I just knew that wasn't me, but I didn't know if this was a battle I could win because I didn't remember anything. I didn't know what the hell I did or was forced to do. I knew I was not gay but if I made accusations against Brown and Morris and they claimed I was gay it would be my word against the Staff Sergeant, and if it came down to the uniform code of military justice then he would be part of the UCMJ system, sitting in judgement on me!

I stepped gingerly into the shower and turned the faucets on as hot as I could bear it to try to wash away the filth and the unjustified but overwhelming sense of shame. I winced as the soapy water stung my wounds. I ignored the shooting pain as I washed and washed, and the swirling water around my feet turned pink, but no amount of scrubbing would expunge the feeling of disgust. I laid low for the rest of the day, nursing my wounds and keeping myself to myself, but my memories – or lack of them – continued to torment me. Had Brown taken photos? I didn't remember seeing any camera but if he and Morris were trying to frame Johnson and me as gay, wouldn't they have wanted some evidence? Was that what they were trying to do – frame us? Had they got Johnson and me naked, done terrible shit to us and then tried to make it looks like it was Johnson and me trying to get everyone involved in gay sex so they could get us kicked out of the military? Or was it just some sick game to humiliate us? Or were Brown and Morris gay? I had no answers and I was not about to ask the sick bastards who had attacked me. I kept going over the brutality of what they had done. I wasn't just raped. I was drugged and had the shit kicked out of me. And when I wasn't torturing myself over the gaps in my knowledge I was overwhelmed with anger – with myself and with the world – that I had been too naïve to see the warning signs. I was raging with fury that I had allowed myself to be rendered so impotent and that I had not done more to defend myself, never mind that there was nothing I could have done. Worst of all, because of his position, I would never be able to get revenge against Brown - that sick, evil excuse for a human being - and so reclaim some of the sense of self-worth he had stolen from me. He had got away with doing whatever he had done to me and there was nothing I could do. I wanted to scream but I couldn't say a word. Wouldn't ever say a word. Rather than admit my weakness and risk being accused of being gay, I vowed to myself never to tell a living soul what had happened to me. I couldn't know it then but it was a decision that was going to screw up my life. I'll stop short of calling it a death sentence, but it was certainly the death of who Ron Carter was meant to be in life.

And so I carried on. My physical wounds healed, though the mental scars never would. I knuckled down to army work but I was irrevocably changed, even if handling weapons, mastering tactics, and coping with the physical rigours still came naturally and I was still proving my worth. I was forever looking over my shoulder, wondering who was watching me and what they were thinking. Pretty soon after the incident I was promoted to E4 – Specialist – and I was being fast-tracked to become a corporal so that I would be promotable to sergeant and go to NCO school. I kept getting bonuses because I just happened to be good at tests. In the field I was an excellent soldier, but in barracks it was a whole different matter. Pretty soon after the incident I started smoking hash and drinking. I mean, I drank before but not like this. I turned to lots of drinking and lots of hash because, when I wasn't out in the field, soldiering, I just really didn't want to be sober. I hated who I was and what had happened to me. I would go out drinking with some of the lads or we would sit in our rooms smoking the hash from the drinking hole of an empty Mountain Dew can which we had pricked with holes with our insignia badges and which we could crumple up and discard later without arousing any suspicion. The hash helped me to chill, but the drinking would stir a red rage and if anyone got sideways with me then I would get punchy. And in barracks, with the rest of my squad, I was a problem because of that anger just below the surface. It must have been obvious to the powers that be that something had suddenly changed in me. Did they know something about what had happened? I certainly have no recollection of ever seeing Brown again. Or Morris. Or Johnson for that matter, but that didn't mean I didn't live in fear and intimidation, dreading seeing my attackers again; terrified of being accused of being gay and kicked out of the Army. Had Johnson reported what had happened and been moved? Had Brown and Morris been moved, or was it that I was not around as much? The chain of command certainly started giving me all sorts of extra work, as well as increasing the duties I already had, which meant I was away from my unit a lot of the time. I was already the M60 gunner for my fire-team, but now they sent me off to Italy to take part in an M60 competition and I won an award - an army achievement medal – for being able to take apart and put back together a 60 in record time, blindfolded. Whenever we went to the live fire ranges they would separate me from my unit, putting me on special assignment to fire all the M47 Dragon ground-to-ground anti-tank missiles because I was the only one who would hit the target every single time. The thing with the Dragon was that it had a huge back-blast area and, firing it from your shoulder, you had to put your collar up and wear a glove or you would get burned. It was wire-guided and accurate to at least a thousand metres but once you fired it you had to hold the sight on target until it hit and most people, when it fired, would flinch really badly and the missile would plough straight into the ground. Bearing in mind this was a $20,000 missile and there would be top brass watching these live fire training events, the chain of command didn't want to have the generals witnessing $20,000 going to dirt! The extra weapons work didn't seem so unusual, maybe, but it felt like I was always in the field, or off-base, and rarely with my unit. That was until the time I was stopped from leaving barracks at all.

Dani had joined the military herself a little while after Gary and me and now she had been posted to Germany. Her mom and grandmother - 'Babe' and 'Corky' - were flying to Germany to visit her and the three of them, and Gary, were going to meet up with me for a 'family' reunion. I was really looking forward to it. The Combs really were the loveliest people I had ever met - a Godsend in my life. And then I got popped for drug use. I was called for a pee-test and because of the THC (cannabis) in my system, I failed and it was a big deal. It meant an immediate Battalion level punishment – a field grade Article 15 – and I was knocked down two ranks. It was effectively three ranks because I had been on the verge of making corporal and now I was back down to Private (E2). They immediately took half of my pay, which was reduced anyway because I was a private again, and I was restricted to post for at least 30 days. It might even have been 45. It was like being in prison. I could go to the chow hall, and go to the barracks to carry out any training they assigned to me, but otherwise I could not go anywhere, and once the day's work was done and I had had my evening meal they would have me report for extra bullshit duties, like mopping floors, until 9pm or later when they were done with me. Confined to barracks, I had to ring Dani and tell her I was in trouble and wouldn't be able to meet her and her family, which really sucked. I wasn't too emotional about it. Basic training, as it was designed to do, had knocked a lot of the emotions out of me and turned me into an orders-follower, but it hurt because I knew how disappointed they would be with me.

It wasn't like I was the only one smoking hash. Lots of people did. They would get it from the Turkish guys in town who were always asking if we wanted any. I said 'No', like forever, but people had it in the barracks. It wasn't as if there was a strong chance of getting caught because they didn't do the pee-tests very often, and they were randomised – or at least I always thought so. But my name came up and I got popped. I quit the hash after that because I knew I would go to jail if I got caught again and I didn't want to get kicked out of the Army. I wanted to stay in. I didn't want to fail. But I knew I could drink so I did lots of that. In the meantime, the work away from my unit just increased. They put me on gate guard duties for three months which meant I was in barracks the whole time but not in the field. I just had to have really nice BDUs and polished boots and check the ID of everyone coming on post. Then they sent me away for Platoon Confidence Training (PCT) for a month with the Special Forces based down at Bad Tolz, near the Austrian border, at the foot of the Alps. Twice. The first time was a real shock. It was winter and super snowy and the training was gruesome – worse even than basic training. The different battalions would hand-pick who they sent there and it was, like, 'send us your bad-asses and we'll put them through the toughest exercises, the toughest land-nav, and the toughest PT'. I was still in pretty good shape and good on the cross-country runs, even in full BDU and boots in the ice and the snow, but I remember one kid who came in some time after me on one particular run and he was bitching about needing water and this huge black E7 (Sergeant First Class) Special Forces dude in the green beret – he must have been at least 6' 7" – picked him up by the throat, with all his gear on, and just took another step forward and body-slammed him down on the ground on his back, then emptied a whole five gallon drum of water over him, virtually water-boarding him, and that was before the terrified lad was made to do the 'Koala Bear', trying to cling upside down on the flag pole which was so slippery with ice that he kept sliding down and landing on his head. On another occasion we did a five-day navigation exercise, with virtually no sleep, trying to evade capture. Luckily my fire team and I never got caught but those who did, we were told, were put in Viet Cong-style below-ground pits with barred lids, too low to stand up in but with freezing water in the bottom so you couldn't sit down. I don't know how long they were kept in there but it was apparently until they were close to hypothermia. The second time I was sent for PCT with the Special Forces was in spring but it wasn't much easier.

Was I being punished, fast-tracked for promotion again, or just being kept out of the way? I had no idea. No one tells you why you are doing any of that stuff. You just do what you're told. I can't remember ever seeing Brown again – and I certainly would not have wanted to - but that might have been because I was not around much on base or because my brain has blocked those memories out, but at the time my efforts to blot out what had happened to me weren't working too well. I didn't have the hash to calm me down and when I went out drinking, I rarely strayed far from base, usually just going to the Irish bar opposite the barracks. But the alcohol with which I used to self-medicate, and try to forget the rape, can't have been working too well because by then the night terrors had started. I would wake in a cold sweat from dreams where I knew I was asleep and could sense someone sneaking up on me to kill me but I could not make myself wake up. In my sleep I would try to scream for help and be unable to make a sound. It was terrifying, and being awake did not always stop the nightmares. My life had become very dark and I just wanted the misery to end but, as a Christian, I told myself that suicide was a sin and would condemn me to Hell. Instead, I dreamed of being involved in medieval combat, slashing and scything my way through enemy forces with a vicious sabre, then being killed in battle with a sword, redeeming myself with a hero's death. And in my waking hours, unable to escape my torment, or the anger within me, I desperately wanted not to be in barracks. I prayed for war so that I could be in the thick of it, killing people. Or getting killed.

CHAPTER SEVEN

An explanation of Post Traumatic Stress Disorder by Dr. Jay McNeil, Principal Clinical Psychologist at Lancashire Teaching Hospitals NHS Foundation Trust, United Kingdom.

Most people that I see who are struggling with the symptoms of trauma are also battling with fear that they are going mad because they don't know why they have these symptoms, so it is important to understand what trauma actually is and why it happens. There are plenty of things generally regarded as traumatic that we would expect to bring on the symptoms of trauma, such as war, disasters, physical violence, sexual violence or sudden or unexpected loss, but many people experience these and are psychologically fine, while some people experience events that others would not find traumatic and suffer the symptoms of trauma, so the event itself is not the critical factor. There are other reasons why someone ends up experiencing the symptoms of a trauma response. Key to whether we develop any difficulties around trauma is our interpretation of what has happened. If we have felt at risk, or seen others at risk, if we've felt powerless, if we've felt unable to cope, these are all things that increase the likelihood of an event being traumatic. So what is trauma? Well, it's a normal response that we have to an abnormal threatening event. Most people will feel traumatised to some degree by something that threatens their life, for example. In these situations it is perfectly normal to have complex distressing feelings. Our trauma response has been present for a long time, and it evolved with a simple purpose: to keep us safe. When something threatening happens we tend to go into a set number of possible responses – fight, flight, freeze, and sometimes fawning. These are to some extent pre-programmed in us, and they tend to take a lot of training and experience to overcome. So what's the reason for them? Why do we have these responses? Well, if you imagine it's thousands of years ago and you're out on the savannah hunting and suddenly a lion rushes at you. What happens if you go 'Oh look, a lion, I'm going to pet it?' Yes, it's gonna eat your face off, and you won't survive to pass on your genes. If however you run away, fight, or even freeze (which, from an evolutionary perspective is the same as playing dead, which is seen in lots of prey mammals) you're more likely to survive and procreate. So the genes that make you more likely to do one of those responses get passed on and those that make you want to pet it don't, so that response dies out. This is hugely simplified, but you get the picture.

So how does this happen? If you understand the neurobiology of it (it's not as complex as it sounds) then the symptoms make more sense. I like to use Dan Siegel's hand model of the brain to explain, because it's nice and simple. If you hold up your hand, nice and flat, with the palm facing towards you and the thumb tucked in, then you can imagine that your arm is the spinal cord and the bottom of your hand, where it meets your wrist, is the brain stem - our 'lizard brain'. The thumb represents our middle brain, with the lowest knuckle of the thumb as something called the amygdala and the top knuckle as something called the hippocampus. If you then fold your fingers down over your thumb, then they represent the brain's outer layer - the cerebral cortex, with the tips of your middle fingers as the prefrontal cortex. Are you with me so far? Good. So, the 'reptile brain' controls the body's automatic functions, like breathing, heartbeat, etc.,that keep us alive. The middle brain, represented by our thumb, is more complex. This is where our emotions are, our fear centre, stress, our responses to the environment that also happen automatically. Our cortex, represented by our fingers and the back of our hand is where our rational brain sits - our thinking, sense of *ourself, where we make decisions, plan and solve problems. When that lion rushes at us, a couple of really critical things happen. Firstly, our senses - in this case our eyes that see the lion coming for us and/or our ears that hear it roar - send this information to our brain. In the middle of our brain is something like a control centre that is constantly, 24/7 monitoring information from our senses, and putting it together to make sense. It's always cross checking the information coming in with our vast stores of knowledge about our previous experiences. Our control centre sees this information of a lion rushing at us and combines it with our previous experiences (maybe a memory of someone else being attacked by a lion), or our knowledge of the world, that lions are dangerous. This happens literally instantaneously. So our control centre recognises this is a threat. It responds in two ways. The most immediate is to activate our response in the middle of the brain. Our hippocampus, a tiny little seahorse shaped bit of brain that usually helps us make memories reduces that function, and puts all its energy into flooding us with stress hormones like adrenalin and cortisol. These pump up our muscles, diverting blood from digestion and non-essential states to the things we might need to escape or fight, like our lungs and heart. Our heart and breathing speed up, so we have enough oxygen for action. Our senses become hyper attuned, so our control centre starts receiving HUGE and detailed data from our senses, and has to try to make sense of that. And all of this takes nanoseconds – it's barely measurable. So fast, indeed, that all this happens before the second thing that our control centre does can even start. And that is important because the second thing that our control centre does is to send a message to the outside layer – the cortex of the brain. Here is where we can make a rational decision, weigh up the pros and cons, and then take action. In a survival situation, a rational response is too slow, which is why we have this automatic process. That can kick in to keep us alive long enough to then decide what else to do.*

This is our brain's natural trauma response. It's a normal reaction to danger and is something that our brain has been getting better and better at for thousands of years. It's kept us as a species alive, and kept any of us who've been in sudden danger alive. So if this is such a natural response and exactly what the brain has evolved to do, how does this become a problem, and why?

Well, for some people, especially those in chronically stressful situations, this mechanism becomes almost jammed on and there's a really good reason for this. Usually, when things happen in our daily life, our brain essentially puts a date stamp on it, and files it away in our memory. So when we remember the experience later we have a sense of it being in the past, of when it happened in relation to our lives now. We know it's over. During a traumatic situation, however, our senses are wide open and flood the brain with tons of information trying to give our control centre anything that can help it help us survive. We can't possibly integrate all that information into a coherent, sensible memory. It's just too much data, so we get snapshots, and fragments. At the same time, the parts of our brain that usually encode memory as being in the past, and give it a date stamp, are busy trying to deal with all of this. So the experience doesn't get filed as in the past. As far as our brain is concerned it's still happening, even after it's stopped. Even though the information we receive after the event is that we're safe, all the other information about danger is still floating around in there, and our brain doesn't know what to do. So any little thing can spark off the full danger response – the bang of a car door, someone walking into a room unexpectedly. If something shares features similar to some of those that were present at the time of the trauma, it's more likely to trigger the response. What's difficult is that some of these triggers won't even be known to the person. So someone's brain might have noticed a red scarf on someone at a mass shooting, but the person won't be aware of it – they were too busy running away, but it was part of all the info from their senses that was flooding their brain. Later they see a red scarf and without knowing why, they're in full panic. And the brain is programmed to keep us safe, so it then thinks a red scarf is dangerous and starts to try to find other things that share similar features, because they might also be dangerous, and before you know it, anything red sets off this response, and the person still doesn't even know what in their environment is making them panic, they just feel panicky - suddenly and out of the blue - a lot of the time. The brain is doing what it's meant to do, it's trying to help, only the danger has passed and what the person needs is for it to calm down.

It's important to think of our response to trauma as being on a scale. It's not that we're either traumatised or we aren't. We have a lot of different reactions to greater or lesser extents to difficult and challenging situations. We might be completely unphased at one end of the scale, to having full blown PTSD at the other. It's normal at first, following exposure to an event that has the potential to traumatise, to have a lot of the following symptoms, which hopefully will make sense now you understand what's happening in the brain. There are four main categories of symptoms:

Re-experiencing. This is the brain trying to make sense of the stimulation it's received. If you think of all the fragments from our senses as being imprinted on jigsaw pieces, and these have all been thrown up in the air and landed in a mess, it's our brain repeatedly sorting through them trying to get them into a coherent picture – a story that makes sense – so it can file it away. So to do that it brings out fragments of experience, bits of memory, seemingly randomly. These might be things the person finds themselves thinking which are unpleasant but which they can put aside, or it might be a full blown flashback, where the person feels exactly as if they are back in that moment having that experience. It can happen during sleep too, usually in the form of nightmares.

Hyper-arousal. If the body is full of stress hormones, it's on full alert so the person can react to the slightest thing. It may be that those hormones are constantly circulating or that it takes a lot less than usual to trigger them, but the end result is the same. The person is edgy, constantly monitoring what's happening around them for danger, having a whole load of physical symptoms like dry mouth, sweaty palms, racing heart. This can obviously stop people being able to sleep, so they can be exhausted but still unable to relax. The less sleep someone has the less able they are to function and manage their emotions, which causes more stress, and so they are less likely to sleep. They can get stuck in a cycle of fatigue.

Avoidance. Because memories or thoughts of what happened can be so distressing, the person may avoid anything that might trigger them. So someone who has been sexually assaulted may avoid people with the same name, or who look similar. The problem with avoidance is that memories, thinking about it, etc. are all important for processing, to help the brain finally file it away. Avoidance stops that happening. In the short term, avoiding reminders of the event temporarily makes the person feel a bit better than if they were always reminded of it, but it actually makes it worse in the long term.

Finally, negative beliefs can occur. We function in the world by assuming some crucial things – that the world is generally a safe place, that people are generally to be trusted or at least not dangerous, and that we are in control of what happens to us. A traumatic event throws all of these up in the air, it completely destabilises our world view. We need those assumptions in order to function. If we felt the world was generally extremely unsafe, that people were inherently dangerous and that we had no control over our lives, we'd never function. Sadly, that's what trauma shows us. We live in a sort of self-imposed ignorance, and traumatic events show us that all is not as we believe. Bad things can still happen. So trauma can lead to people's beliefs about themselves, others and the world being re-shaped and re-defined.

These core symptoms, continuing for a certain period of time, are *the classic features of a medical diagnosis of PTSD. Many people will have all of these in the initial days after a traumatic event, but when they don't ease, and are interfering with a person's ability to function months later, they are likely to attract a diagnosis of PTSD. Along with these symptoms, there are also other things that people are likely to experience. These include problems with anger, anxiety, depression and sleep. They may be extremely irritable, and find themselves lashing out at those around them. Or they might withdraw from those who are trying to help. Some can withdraw so much that they detach from reality, or dissociate. In extreme examples of this, they may find themselves missing time. People can have a huge range of emotions in response, such as fear, grief, loss, humiliation, shame and guilt. The feelings and memories of trauma may be so unbearable that they turn to drugs or alcohol to try to get away from them, or self-harm. One of the most common ways people try to address nightmares and sleep problems is by using alcohol. Unfortunately this actually causes significant disruption to our sleep patterns. The type of sleep we have after alcohol is not the same as normal sleep, and over time this increases the likelihood of nightmares, so people can become stuck in a cycle of needing more and more alcohol. Ironically, nightmares are one of the easiest symptoms of trauma to treat. People who are hyper aroused can't concentrate well, they don't remember things because they aren't paying attention, and sleep problems also make this worse. Not everyone who experiences a potentially traumatising event will be traumatised, and still fewer will have PTSD, but for those who do develop these symptoms - and they are distressing, unmanageable, or not getting any better - it is essential to seek medical help. PTSD Is very treatable, but it's easier and quicker to treat when it's addressed rapidly. The longer you leave it, the harder it is.*

To summarise, trauma isn't just over when the event has finished. It can alter a person's emotional and psychological state and change their physiology. As well as the individual, it can affect their relationships with those around them through problems with trust or intimacy. It can impair their employment, their ability to function in the world. It reaches out much further than just the day the event happened, or the place it occurred. It can change everything, but that isn't always all bad. For some people, trauma can lead to a phenomenon called post-traumatic growth. This is where the person processes what has happened to them and is able to come out of trauma stronger, more resilient, and more secure in themselves than they were before. Trauma makes us re-evaluate everything, and sometimes that can make positive change happen, that enhances a person's life. It's not that they are happy the trauma happened necessarily, but given that it has and they can't change that, they've taken what they can from it to grow and improve their lives. As with trauma, not everyone has the tools, support, or resources to be able to do that, and so if someone doesn't experience growth it doesn't mean there's something wrong with them. But with the right help, it is possible.

CHAPTER EIGHT

The road seemed endless and as desolate as it was monotonous as it carved its way through the featureless desert. Numerous white crosses beside the highway, each commemorating the death of a previous traveller, added to the sense of foreboding as we maintained a steady 55mph and they flashed past my periphery vision. Little wonder that they call this forlorn highway the longest cul-de-sac in the world, and as we neared my new base I sensed more than ever that I and my Army career were heading for a dead end. I had been mentally scarred by my time in Germany but worse was to follow. Promoted back to Private First Class (E3), I had been looking forward to a fresh start when my two-year foreign posting came to an end and I was due a Permanent Change of Station (PCS) back to the US. Instead, I found that my regiment's time in Germany was also ending and that the entire unit was returning to the US at the same time, to the same base as me. I would still be with the 1/52 and all the emotional baggage from Bamberg would be posted home with me. As if that was not bad enough, our new base was the National Training Center at Fort Irwin, in the middle of the Mojave Desert, one of the hottest places on earth, more than 30 miles from the nearest town. Turning off Interstate 15 at Barstow, on to Fort Irwin Road, the barren landscape in every direction reflected the emptiness I felt inside. Linear white clouds painted abstract pictures in the big blue sky above, but at ground level there were just sandy plains and the occasional cactus. A light breeze threw up dust devils that danced across the white line at the centre of the thin asphalt strip that stretched arrow-like directly ahead towards the jagged silhouette of the Sierra Nevada far in the distance. The straightest section - known for some reason as '10-Mile Stretch' - seemed to go on for at least twice that length before we reached the only discernible landmark on the 31-mile route – a rainbow coloured patchwork of stones known as 'Painted Rock' where the many units which had preceded us at Fort Irwin had crafted their insignias, presumably to let those who followed know they had been there...and had escaped. The rock signalled that we were finally close to our destination, and as we rounded a corner a collection of tan buildings surrounded by miles of wire fencing that was the perimeter of Fort Irwin appeared on the high desert valley below. We had arrived.

The base had decent facilities for staff and for serving personnel with families, set up in accommodation villages, but for single soldiers it was still just another barracks on a wildly remote posting, which was not great for someone with so much going on inside his head and too much time to think. I was still getting the night terrors and, like too many people with undiagnosed PTSD, using alcohol in a mistaken bid to help myself sleep. There were no bars where enlisted men could drink - even if I had been old enough when we first arrived. There was just a bar for the NCOs and a bar for the officers. That didn't mean I couldn't get a drink on post when training was done for the day, or at the weekends. I could and I did – regularly, and much more than I should have done - to mask the emotions that were bedevilling me. We would usually get some beers from the grocery store and drink at someone's house or in the barracks. Our supply Sergeant would also hold card games at his married quarters on post and we would drink a lot there while we played spades. Occasionally we would take the 40 minute drive to Barstow in search of beer and sex but the Barstow women were not into army guys and the fake ID I had acquired in order to get served drink led to my next brush with the military authorities. Inevitably I was caught with it getting back on post. That could have been an Article 105a offence under the UCMJ. I was lucky not to have faced charges again but it was another red flag for me.

I'm pretty certain that neither Brown nor Morris was assigned back to Fort Irwin but, with my undiagnosed PTSD playing havoc with my brain, I nevertheless sensed threats everywhere that I looked and I was ready to fight anyone, anytime, rather than ever let someone humiliate me again. Despite my drinking I was still in good physical shape and, for the second time in my life, I set about making myself into someone that no one would want to mess with. I lifted weights, got tattoos and fought anyone who so much as looked at me the wrong way, and in the testorerone-fueled environment of a military base there were plenty of contenders. It was mostly just meaningless scraps and the rest of the time I was still pretty sociable and I

got lucky on my 21st birthday. There was a Hispanic guy in my unit who had the exact same birthday as me and the two of us made the journey to a bar in Barstow to celebrate being able to drink legally. The pretty bar-tender liked our birthday story and seemed to like me even more, so when I was paying the bill she handed me a rubber, a phone number and instructions on where and when to meet her when she finished work. So I did. On other occasions when we had more time off, usually after a long rotation in the field, I and a few other guys would go to Los Angeles or Las Vegas, or rent a house in Hermosa Beach, California, and get hammered for days on end. Those breaks presented more opportunities for me to try to put what had happened behind me, but the rage was still inside and even then I would avoid getting blind drunk because I was terrified of being unconscious, at the mercy of whoever might attack me.

Spring rolled into summer and the temperatures in the desert soared, often over 120 degrees. The conditions were oppressive enough even without the dust-filled wind which funnelled down the nearby Death Valley in the late afternoon and felt like someone blowing a hair dryer in your face. It put everyone on edge. You just had to hope each day that training would be in an air conditioned building, not out in the field, and in the evening you tried to relax and keep cool as best you could. That's how I came to be drinking one particular weekday night, by invitation, at an event in the NCO bar. I didn't drink a ton – maybe four or five beers - but it was clearly enough to stir the PTSD monster inside me, so when I got back to the third floor room in the barracks that I shared with two other guys I was in no mood to be messed with. It was already dark, around 10pm, but the temperature was still in the high 80s. I just wanted to watch some trashy TV then try to get to sleep, if my night terrors allowed, but one of my roomies – I'll call him Garcia - was watching my TV when I got back and he refused to change the channel. He was a small dude, but mouthy with it, and something of a karate guy, as he loved to tell people. We exchanged some expletive-laden words but when he still refused to let me change the channel I grabbed him and threw him out of the room, then locked the door after him, leaving him standing in the stairwell in his underwear, banging on the door and yelling abuse. I simply switched the channel on my TV, turned up the volume and lay on my bunk to watch it until Garcia stopped banging on the door. A short while later my other roomie, whose bunk was closer to the window, told me that Garcia was out the front, shouting for everyone in the barracks to hear that I was a 'pussy' and a 'coward' and that he was calling me out. I had a decision to make. 'Should I go out there and kick his ass?' I asked my buddy. 'Damn right,' he replied. 'If he's idiot enough to call you out in front of more than 300 men then you can't ignore it.' Status and your place in the pecking order were a big thing in the military and determined how others treated you, so failing to respond when challenged was not an option. Even as I made my way down the three flights of stairs I could hear Garcia shouting at the top of his lungs for me to face him or let everyone know I was a 'faggot'. It was the sort of incident that would often draw a crowd but there was no one else outside. Perhaps it was just too hot for them to be bothered, or maybe a few of them were simply watching from their windows to see what the fuss was about and keeping well out of it. If they were, they would have seen Garcia still shouting and still gesticulating at me as I ran towards him. I smashed into him at full pelt, then grounded and pounded him until I felt the fight was won and my honour was satisfied. No onlookers could possibly think Ron Carter was a 'pussy' or a 'coward' based on what they had just seen. Nor would anyone think it was OK to touch me, I was sure, so I let him go. But even as he started up the stairs he was still talking shit, giving me abuse for anyone to hear, as if to save face, and that's when I lost it. I ran to catch up with him again, threw him back down the stairs then started pummelling his nuts with my fist as hard as I could because by then the red monster had taken over and knew no limits. Nothing else was in my head other than the thought of hurting the guy for trying to humiliate me. I left him groaning in pain and returned to our room to watch TV. I couldn't have cared less how he was at the time but apparently he went to hospital and spent a few days there until his nuts were no longer swollen to the size of grapefruits. They moved him out of our room after that because I'm pretty sure he was not willing to face me again, knowing how disturbed I was. In the meantime I had to go and see the commander – I'll call him Captain Williams - the next morning and he spelled out in no uncertain terms just how deep in shit I was. I lost rank again – back down to E2 – and a few days later I had to personally apologise to Garcia, whose face was still badly bruised and who was still having trouble walking. It could have been much worse but Captain Williams was an excellent officer. He knew me to be a very good soldier but could see that I was seriously struggling for some reason that I couldn't tell him, so he decided to take me under his wing. He told me that, in order to save me from being kicked out of the military, he was moving me out of my unit into HQ Platoon and making me his driver and that I had better appreciate it or I would be gone.

In Germany we had been stuck with the shitty old Jeeps but the

US Army had just introduced Humvees and I was now driving one of the first. It's fair to say that I loved it. Captain Williams also became a pretty profound mentor in my life. I think he saw something of himself in me and wanted to keep me by his side and out of trouble and I bless him for that. He was just a great human being. He had grown up in a really poor neighbourhood in Boston – I mean dirt poor – and he said both his mother and his brother had mental health issues so from the age of nine or ten he had been the one paying the bills, chasing up their welfare checks and making sure they kept their home because he was bright and disciplined. When it came to school he got straight As, and his teachers and others recognised his talent. He told me that some wealthy family had taken him under their wing and they had a senator friend who gave his backing so that he was recommended for the US Military Academy at West Point, New York, from where he graduated. I'll be forever grateful that at Fort Irwin he was looking out for me because I was still getting into scraps. You know, we were a bunch of young men in tight quarters, trained for combat, and those dust-ups just happened, but with my undiagnosed PTSD prompting my actions I usually took it too far. I was always mortified afterwards because I felt that wasn't who I was, but in those moments the monster inside of me would take over. I had vowed to myself that no one would ever fuck with me again and I was keeping that promise.

My nightmares, about fighting and dying, simply rehearsed those PTSD responses in my sleep and went some way to reinforcing them in my head during waking hours. Fortunately, with Captain Williams doing his best to keep me out of trouble, I got through the rest of the summer and the fall without landing myself in hot water again. Then winter arrived. Christmas came and went with more exercises in the field and so with some time off due in the New Year, a bunch of us took a guided ski trip to Mammoth Mountain, a four and a half hour bus ride to the north in the Sierra Nevada. The skiing was lively and the apres-ski even livelier as we hit the bars of Mammoth Lakes. On the last night I foolishly got into a drinking contest with a buddy and some others back at our hotel. As we downed beer after beer and shot after shot around the fire, the fear I had had since my rape of being unconscious went out of the window. I remembered being annoyed with another room-mate of mine who I had grown not to like. He was a white kid from Detroit who fancied himself as some kind of gangster and regularly talked about killing people and how he had shot gang rivals. It was typical rap talk that likely wasn't true or, at worst, was only partially true. It grated on me when I was sober but as the drink flowed he began talking more and more crap and becoming more and more threatening and I could feel the monster rising. And then I blacked out. I woke up in a cell in the tiny Mono County jail, an hour's drive away, facing felony charges but I had no clue what had happened or how I had got there. I mean, I knew I had to have done something horrific, but what? Fortunately the Sheriff there seemed to take a shine to me because he let me out to use a pay phone and I used my MCI card to call my dad. I had to tell him 'I'm sorry to call but I just got let out of a jail cell and I have no idea what I did,' and he rightly said, 'Well, the best thing you can do is to go back in there and ask them what you did and see what your options are.' So that's what I did. All that the Sheriff would tell me was that I had put someone in hospital but he was chuckling like it was funny and he told me, 'Look, as far as I'm concerned, you're the military's problem. I don't want you as my problem,' and he put me in his car and gave me a ride back to Mammoth Lakes. It turned out that I had lost it with the mouthy room-mate and beaten the crap out of him but I only found that out because Captain Williams had made everyone involved write up a report about what had happened and I had to read them. I had laid into the guy and broken his ribs which had lacerated his liver or his spleen, so he was in a bad way and would be in hospital for a little while. Our tour guide's wife had popped her head out of their room at the height of the commotion and I had told her to get back in her room or I would kill her, and I punched her husband when he got involved. Apparently I also punched a cop, who had been called to the disturbance, and a Staff Sergeant. When the Sheriff got me back to Mammoth Lakes in time for the bus home, the same Staff Sergeant sat next to me to make sure I didn't attack anybody else, although I was sober by then and had no intention of hitting anybody. All I wanted to do was cry.

Captain Williams was understandably pissed with me. 'I should kick you out of the military, right?' he yelled at me. 'You should be dishonourably discharged.' He called me a son-of-a-bitch and worse and he was steaming mad and I don't blame him, but he didn't know what had happened to me in Germany and I wasn't about to tell him. None of it was an excuse to do the things that I did but I wasn't mentally stable. I wasn't right. I'm sure I lost rank again but by then I didn't care. My time in the military was coming to an end. I know I should have made sergeant in Germany, given how good I was at soldiering in the field, but my behaviour after the rape had killed off any chances of that. I probably should have got kicked out of the Army, as Captain Williams said, after the Mammoth incident, but thanks to him I wasn't. Instead he ordered me to take the physical and exams for flight school. He told me, 'Look, if you re-enlist, I will send you to the Army Aviation Center of Excellence at Fort Rucker, Alabama, and you will become a Warrant Officer and fly helicopters.' I passed the physical with ease but I didn't bother to study for the exam. I just turned up and took it. As it happened, I scraped through and could have gone but Bill Clinton was in the process of shrinking the size of the military and I had already decided to take the option to leave over becoming a helicopter pilot and it would prove to be one of the biggest regrets of my life.

CHAPTER NINE

Testimony Of Us Marine Corps Female Veteran 'A' - Twice Sexually Assaulted By Ncos:

The first time it happened it was by my First Sergeant which is pretty high up there in rank – like the second highest you can go in enlisted ranks – and I was a lowly young Lance Corporal working directly under him. I was 22 at the time, with just a couple of years of service and he was just one step below Sergeant Major – so five ranks above me – and maybe in for 25 years and I had been raised not to speak up against my superiors. My dad was super strict and I grew up with the ethos 'You don't question, you don't say 'No', you just do what you are told without asking questions, so I was groomed for the military. I was perfect for it. That's why I did so well. I did not ever ask questions. I just did what I was told. And the First Sergeant was a very intimidating person. He was infantry, a huge black dude, and scary, always screaming at people. The First Sergeant serves as the senior enlisted Marine in the company, assisting in the unit's administration, morale and Marine welfare matters and it was his job to discipline people and keep them in line. You know, if you got into trouble it was the First Sergeant you got sent to, and I was his clerk. He was also the person in charge of doing health and comfort inspections, so he would come into our rooms. We would be told, 'You have 24 hours to get your room ready for a health and comfort inspection' and he would come into our barracks rooms and he would go through everything, all our drawers, all of our cabinets, looking for paraphernalia like drugs, alcohol, guns or whatever we might have in our rooms that they didn't think we should have. So it was 2002 and he came to my room one time and, going through my drawers, he found a vibrator because I was a single gal and I think he thought that meant, like, 'Oh, she's...' I don't know what he thought but I try to reason with myself. I think we all do, I guess, desperately wondering 'What could I have done to prevent this? Did I lead him on in any way?' Anyway, I had to stand in the hallway while he inspected my room and he found it and came out with it and asked, 'Oh, what's this? Do I need to confiscate this?' you know, and so he immediately made me feel uncomfortable and it was already not OK. I was working for him for a while and he would take his clerks out to lunch every so often and he took me out to lunch one day and he knew I was looking for a house in the same area where he was living and so when we went out for lunch he was like, 'Oh, let's just swing by my house. I will show you my neighbourhood since you're looking in this area,' and I didn't feel able to say 'No' so I was like, 'Er...' and off we go.

It happened at his house and I just froze. It was like I did not have any control over my body because I was so afraid of what would happen afterwards and if I was just still and didn't do anything it would be over and I could go. I remember one thing during it – I saw a picture of his wife on the wall in his bedroom and all I could think was 'What the fuck is happening right now?' I disassociated from my body. It was almost like I did not have any power or control. Afterwards he was, like, 'If you ever say anything to anyone your life is over. I will ruin you.' I ended up getting pregnant but I could not go to the base medical center because they make you take a test and it goes on your record, so there was no privacy. You had to ask your commanding officer if you could have an abortion. I don't know what it's like now but back then you had to request permission to get married or anything like that and who you ask...is the First Sergeant! So I would have had to go to this person and say, 'Hey, I am pregnant, what are we going to do?' I was at the Marine Corps base in Quantico, Virginia, and since I could not go to my own medical center I had to go to Baltimore and find this shady abortion clinic and because I could not afford much I got the cheapest procedure possible and it was basically these pills and it kills the baby and you have to just let it come out so that's what I did. I dealt with that all on my own. I did not have family in the area, I did not tell anyone. I did not even tell my parents.

Like I said, the First Sergeant was married but I don't think that I was the only one he raped. There was another girl who I was roommates with for a bit in the barracks and I think that she, you know, I think she had some issues with him too. We didn't talk about it. She alluded to being afraid of him and not wanting to be around him and all that.

And then it happened again, a year later when I was working as a military police officer, as a 911 emergency dispatcher, and this time it was a Staff Sergeant who was the duty officer in charge, checking posts, and I was on duty. I was not raped that time but I was sexually assaulted. This man was checking my post where I worked alone and he forced me to give him a blow job. After it was over I was like, 'Oh fuck, why didn't I try...I should have just bit his dick off,' but in the moment...if only you could have that clarity. Instead, you just let it happen and think, 'It will be over and then I don't have to suffer any more.' After that I tried anything I could to get out of working in his office and I moved to the NCIS (Naval Criminal Investigative Service) buying drugs under cover and that led me down a really bad path. The most natural way to get people talking is by smoking and so I started smoking and drinking heavily and generally abusing my body. I confused sex with love and went from bad relationship to bad relationship. If men wanted to have sex with me it felt at least like some kind of intimacy. After that it was just abusing myself, taking away the feeling. I had ten years after that in the military – so 12 in all – and it was failed relationship after failed relationship. I was married and divorced four times, including to the father of my son who was born in 2005, and I'm sure it affected the way I raised my son. At times it was easier for me to tell him 'No' than do anything *that would trigger bad memories. Both of my attackers had been black men and I could not stand to be around black men. Also, I could not sit with my back to a door. I still can't do that in a restaurant or anything. I also carry a gun with me everywhere I go. It's OK in Arizona because anyone can carry and you don't have to have a licence, but it has affected my safety. I never feel safe. I never feel I can trust anyone... or myself because I allowed that to happen.*

But I carried on with my life and my career and I was going to re-enlist and do another four years but they gave me this physical because I wanted to be a physical training instructor, and they said, 'Your knees are shot. You are not fit for service. We are going to medically retire you.' But in order to do that they put you through all sorts of tests and questions to make sure you are ready for civilian life and they put me through this PTSD questionnaire. They asked me if I had PTSD and I said, 'No, I've never been in combat,' but they gave me this test with something like 300 questions and they said, 'You have PTSD – badly.' I was highly alert, suffered nightmares, anxiety and depression. My life was a rollercoaster all the time. So I had to tell them what had happened to me. I had to report the whole dynamic about how it happened and relive all the embarrassment. It was an all-male unit I was in, because females were not allowed in combat then, so I felt so alone. They already thought I should not be there. I got told that on a regular basis. Half of the men in the military did not want you there. It was embarrassing. I just wanted to get the fuck out of it. They rated me 100% disabled based on my PTSD, but I had to fight for that for two years. I did some research and a lot of people with PTSD present as having borderline personality disorder. You are low, low, low and then something happens and it is a peak and you live your life like you are on cocaine 24/7 and then you crash again and that's what my life was like. Scientifically, people who have ever suffered trauma have borderline personality disorder. And they give you drugs for personality disorder. That is why a lot of people kill themselves. You don't need the drugs. You need therapy. So I got out and realised I was not living with it (the sexual assaults) as a truth. I had not dealt with anything, and it doesn't get easier.

My ex-husband, to whom I was married for seven years, was an abusive, alcoholic narcissist and he would guilt trip me if I would not have sex with him, which is the worst thing you can do to a rape victim. It's only in the last couple of years I have started looking into what's wrong inside myself. Another thing is how the universe kind of puts things in your way to make you check your triggers. Both of my attackers were African-Americans. Well, my mum married a black man – a Jamaican - after that and now I have this whole side of my family that is black and I have two brothers now and they are both very aggressive males and they are Jamaican, so it is, like 'OK, this is a new challenge. The universe is putting this in my way because I need to …it is like a mirror for me. This is what I have to work on – not all black men are dangerous and not all black men are out to hurt you.' I've only started to deal with it, with my PTSD, in the last few years but a big thing for me is people talking about military service and disability and all this other stuff and they question my PTSD because I did not deploy or go to war, so it's like, 'Oh, is my PTSD less than those guys who got shot at because I did not go to combat?' and that's why I don't usually talk about it, especially with other veterans who don't understand. They think, 'Well, you didn't go to combat. You don't have PTSD.' Well, I had a part of me taken away and it makes me feel weak. I have been a single mum for almost 18 years, and was in the Marine Corps and I can take care of myself and I take care of my son and I take care of everything and to talk about someone, you know, putting their power over me, it is like, I dunno, I just feel like, 'How could I not have protected myself?' But they were both superiors and in the military that is a big deal. I think the biggest thing for me is the child. I think about that more than anything – the fact that I had that child inside of me and I couldn't bring myself to have it, or raise it, and I feel bad. I always wonder, 'What might that child have become?' I just wonder what he – I think it was a boy – might have become. But then maybe I would not have had my son, who I adore.

RON CARTER

CHAPTER TEN

The sudden violent movement threatened to pull me off my feet and send me sprawling but I stiffened my sinews and braced myself ready for the fight. My adversary was certainly up for it. As the line went as taut as piano wire, my rigger-gloved hands gripped my fishing rod tightly and, with my tanned muscles bulging, I took the strain and prepared for a long battle with the game fish on the other end. Then I turned to my dad with the biggest of grins. It had seemed like the longest time since I had laughed so freely.

I took a few months off after leaving the military and it was the perfect antidote to the turmoil I had been going through. My dad had, by then, been divorced by my first step mom – the horse lady – who had met a vet, and Dad was living on a 34ft boat in a San Diego marina and I hooked up with him for the rest of the spring and early summer. He never let on to me how badly he had been affected by the break-up of his marriage - I only found that out later – but I guess the fun we had was good for both of us at the time. Mostly we did a ton of fishing and enjoyed the freedom for a while. We would regularly go out into the Mexican waters and catch game fish, like marlin, sailfish or yellowtail, or we would catch huge rohita and sea bass, and at night we would camp on the beach and barbeque some of our haul. The rest we gave away to the local villagers and there was a whole bunch of it. We would explain to the local kids that all this catch – like around 40lbs of fish meat at a time – was for them and their families and they would take it back to their village and their moms would almost always make fish tacos for us, so we would have our dinner made for us and we'd feed a village at the same time, so it was super cool. I was still drinking a lot in the evenings, though it didn't seem so messed up while we were living such a relaxed lifestyle, and the nightmares had eased a little. Sooner or later, however, the good times had to come to an end. I had to go learn how to be a man. Obviously the military had helped to teach me some lessons about life – some of which I wish I had not had to learn – but, to me, becoming a whole, rounded human being meant going to school to get a degree on my way to starting a career. I decided to go back up to Portland, moved in with my mom and started structural fire school at Portland Community College, with a view to becoming a firefighter. Around about the same time, my former colleagues in the military were being mobilised for the Gulf War and it is still a sadness for me that I was in such a head space that I didn't give a shit. I just wanted to be as far away from the military as possible. My best buddy, Gary, had also been deployed to Saudi Arabia and I didn't even communicate with him much. That's how disillusioned I was. I just wanted out. I did join the Oregon Army National Guard, but that was purely because the training was easy for me, I only had to do one weekend a month and it earned me some money to help pay my bills, though my heart was never in it and I didn't enjoy it. I had learned to my cost that, alongside some truly great people, the military is full of pathetic nonentities who would get trodden under foot in civilian life but who, by dint of undeserved rank, get to exert power over others and the military systems make their bullying unquestionable. I had learned, also, that there are too many people who work harder at not working than they would have worked had they done the work they were meant to do. They call it 'shamming' and, as someone with a strong work ethic, I hated it. So I knuckled down to my studies and some extra work too. As well as doing college full-time, I worked 40 hours a week on a ranch belonging to a buddy's millionaire parents – for six bucks an hour, under the table – and at one time I worked as a retail clerk at the GI Joe's clothing stores. I had the GI Bill to pay for my school fees, but I still had a room at my mom's to pay for and had to help with the food and other costs because she had no spare cash. I also had to have my own car and insurance and gas and stuff, so I needed to earn my own money. Despite all the work I did outside of college, I still got good grades. I was a good student and, as I have said, taking exams came easy for me. When I got the time, I also tried to date plenty of girls but that was one test I regularly flunked. Sure, I was fairly witty, decent-looking, I guess, and physically fit, so I got lots of opportunities to date really good women, but I was still messed up inside and always quick to argue. It wasn't that I was consciously thinking about what had happened to me in 'the incident', or my vow never to tell anyone my secret, but I would too often get angsty over trivial things and be ready to fight, and if I had had a drink, which I usually had, it would be worse. I was rowing with everyone – my mom, my sisters, my friends, my girlfriends and whoever I happened to be dating at the time, so the romantic relationships were usually short-lived. It stemmed from my feeling of worthlessness, as a result of my PTSD, and giving everything to make others feel happy, so that when they were not happy I felt like I had failed them but I didn't even know why I was meant to have failed them so I just became defensive and argumentative and when I was triggered I would go off into a red mist rage.

Fighting fires was the way I was going to prove myself, I thought, but the reality of my chosen profession did not live up to the promise. At the end of my two-year college course I did a six-month internship with the Portland Fire Department but that started to make me think that maybe I was not cut out for the job. It was cool enough responding to car accidents and pumping people's chests to save their lives, but I wanted to fight fires – I wanted to be a hero, to salve my feelings of failure - and I don't think that we fought a single fire in the whole six months I was there. More often than not we were responding to EMS (Emergency Medical Service) calls and the vast majority of them were to attend to some little old lady or little old man who was just really lonely. They would forget to take their angina medicine, or whatever, and call on the Fire Department when they fell ill. It occurred to me at the time that Americans are not really good at taking care of our elderly and, in their loneliness, these people would call us out so frequently they knew the firefighters by name and that made me very sad. Not every call was to a regular patient, of course, and it was an unfamiliar address that we responded to on one particular occasion that still haunts me. The adrenaline was pumping as I jumped into the fire truck with my fellow fire fighters and the siren wailed as we sped out of the garage. The word from control was that it was indeed another EMS call but that didn't mean we wouldn't go all out to save whoever needed us. As the inexperienced intern, I was a little nervous as we arrived to find a guy of around 60 who was having a major heart attack. He was seriously obese and I would later learn it was his third heart-attack but that wasn't a concern at that moment. Straight out of college, my CPR skills (cardiopulmonary resuscitation) were as up-to-date as anyone's so I got on with chest compressions and, together with others, we kept him alive long enough to get him to hospital. I followed him as he was wheeled on a gurney into the Emergency Room and watched the ER team shock him with the defibrillator paddles. I felt we had done a decent job – certainly the best we could - but as the effects of my adrenalin began to fade I was acutely aware of the guy's son, who was about my age, standing behind me, crying and pleading for us all to save his dad. It was out of my hands by then but it was gut-wrenching to hear. The

ER team were doing their stuff and we firefighters had to leave so I wasn't there when the doctors cracked open the guy's chest and manually massaged his heart for several minutes until they finally had to admit defeat and confirm his death, but as we drove away I could still hear the son's desperate pleas and cries of anguish ringing in my head and I couldn't shake it off. I'm a very emotional and empathetic person and, to this day, when I recall that incident it brings me to tears, which meant the prospect of being a firefighter for the rest of my life was going to be challenging. Nevertheless, I worked hard to find a job. I took tests at fire departments all over the place – physical agility tests, written exams and oral exams – and I would crush them, but Portland, being a particularly liberal, progressive city, was aggressively implementing Bill Clinton's affirmative action policy at the time and I was their idea of the Antichrist – a white, straight male.

At least the imminent arrival of the summer gave me some respite from the fruitless job-hunting. My then girlfriend, who had been working for a women's clothing store in Portland, had gotten a manager's job for the same chain up in Alaska and she told me, 'I'm gonna take this job and move up there,' so I said, 'Cool, I'll go up there with you.' While she took a flight or two up to Ketchikan, I organised a logging job there for the summer, packed the basics I would need into my stick-shift 1978 Ford F-250 and hit the highway. It was the first time I had done a big road trip by myself like that and I loved it. I drove up through Washington, up through the wilds of British Columbia, Canada, drove on to the car ferry in Prince Rupert and sailed the near 100 nautical miles up the Dixon Entrance to Revillagigedo Island, where the giant trees of Alaska awaited me. The scenery along the way was stunning and it was the perfect young man's adventure. And then the hard work started. The size of the trees up there had to be seen to be believed and I was working six days a week, 13 or 14 hours a day. Physically, the military had been easy by comparison. My girlfriend had rented an apartment in Ketchikan but I was working so many hours I didn't see too much of her, which was probably not a bad thing. We would only have argued because, sadly, that is what we did, especially when I drank, and there was little else to do up there. Ketchikan had more bars per capita than pretty much anywhere in the world, I reckoned, and people there just got drunk, which was not great for a guy with undiagnosed PTSD. I only drank on weekends but the guys logging with me drank every damn day. It was amazing the amount of booze they had. And then one day I watched a couple of guys get killed by a huge root wad. The wires from a tower that were meant to anchor the wad on the steep hillside suddenly pulled free from this stump and the giant root system rolled down the hill and killed two poor loggers who were unlucky enough to get in the way. I quit that day, went back to the apartment and told my girlfriend, 'I'm going back to the States,' and I hit the road again.

Back in Portland I still couldn't get a job to save my life and it didn't matter how many places I applied to and how well I did on their tests, and it was pretty depressing. My girlfriend came back to Oregon not long after. I think she got lonely and wanted to see her family, so we got back together briefly, but it was over pretty quickly. I had probably been traumatized all over again by the accident I witnessed and I didn't want anything to do with the memories of Alaska. I started dating another girl who lived in downtown Portland and it was great while it lasted. I met her at a dance club and she was very stable, super smart with a great job at the bank and if, at that age, I was going to marry anyone it would have been her but I was just terrible at relationships. My fight or flight response would kick in at the least thing and I thought that everyone was out to get me. You know, I tried to be kind and loving and all the things you're meant to be, but then I would get triggered by something and totally over-react. I hated the monster inside of me that would appear with the slightest provocation, so I totally understand why other people would not want to put up with that. I didn't trust myself to be stable marriage material, so why on earth should they? So I just moved on to the next girl. Cynthia and I dated for a couple of months in the late summer and early autumn after I had got back from Alaska but, like with so many of my other relationships, we just broke up. And then, round about October, she called me out of the blue and said, 'Hey, we're gonna have tequila shots – me and my girlfriends – and we want you to come round.' Well I said 'yes' and it was a fun night and, of course, I got drunk and there was no way I could drive so Cynthia insisted, 'You need to stay with me,' so I did. I don't know if she had planned the whole thing from the beginning in order to get me in her bed but that's what happened and the repercussions would hit me later.

CHAPTER ELEVEN

The phone rang a few times before I could reach it and when I did I was surprised to hear Cynthia's voice on the other end of the line. She hadn't been in touch once since the last time we met so whatever that brief liaison over tequila shots had been about she clearly hadn't seen it as the rekindling of any long term relationship, but then nor had I. 'So why is she ringing now?' I wondered. Her tone was matter of fact and I thought that perhaps she was planning another party. Then she dropped the bombshell. She told me she would be having a baby in a month's time and that I would be the dad. 'So why the hell had she not said anything before?' She told me she didn't expect me to stick around and she didn't want any child support. 'You just do what you just do and I will let you know how it goes,' she said. To say I was shocked would be an understatement. Shocked and angry. I felt like I had been used and that I was about to become a father but had no say in it. It was not like, if I had known earlier, I would have said, 'You've got to have an abortion,' or anything like that. Her body was her body, but that was my sperm and my child too. I had already had one child taken from me when I was 18 and so this was another kick in the teeth.

For the eight months since we had met up again I had persevered, fruitlessly, searching for a job as a firefighter but something had to change. Eventually my brother-in-law, who was in advertising and who lived in California's San Francisco Bay Area with my sister, had said, 'Look, you would make a good sales person. Just move down here and live with us and get a sales job,' and so that's what I decided to do. It was just when I was about to move to northern California when Cynthia called and it hit like a bolt of lightning. The worst thing was she was not giving me any kind of choice. I could have forced a choice, I suppose. I could have said, 'Well, guess what? I'm staying here and I'm going to be a father and you're going to let me see my child because you don't just get to get pregnant and tell me to fuck off,' but I definitely was not in that head space at the time. At 35, or 40, I would have been, but at 24 my view was, 'Well, fuck you for not telling me and I'm moving to California and don't come at me for money because if you do I'm going to move back up to Portland and be a father,' which I was pretty sure she didn't want. She had made it absolutely clear that she couldn't give a shit if I was involved in our child's life. In turmoil once again, I carried on with my planned move to California. I made the decision to move on and not stay there and I can't say that that has not been another great regret in my life.

By the time Lindsie was born, a month or so later, I was already living in the Bay Area with my sister and brother-in-law and working as a sales rep for a low-voltage wire and cable company, so I was oblivious to the responsibilities - and the joys - of new parenthood. I simply threw myself into my work and spent my leisure time pumping iron in the gym or drinking at the weekends, and it was a pretty meaningless existence. The gregarious, ambitious young Ron Carter who had joined the military eight years before would not have recognised me at all. Back in Portland I had had a pretty good group of buddies, particularly from the gym, and we would lift all the time then go out and drink and meet girls. It wasn't super sophisticated but at least I had company. Less so in California. I don't know what it is about big cities but it's just hard to make friends if you're not from there, so I didn't, much. I had friends from Portland who would come visit, and I had my sister and brother-in-law that I hung out with when I was staying with them, but I had become a bit of a loner. The only girl I recall dating at that time was a Hispanic woman – Magdalena – but it didn't last long, probably because, with all my issues, I wasn't very kind to her. And of course I got drunk from time to time and I got in fights in bars when the monster raised its head. I tried to pass it off as just the effects of the alcohol, which is easy to do because plenty of people without PTSD behave badly when they're drunk, but looking back now I think my lack of ability to create lasting friendships was due to my hyper-vigilance. A lot of fighting was certainly down to that, and then when you add alcohol that's a really bad recipe for someone with PTSD. It didn't help that my job had me on the road a lot of the time and the horrendous traffic in the Bay Area meant I was always late which, as an ex-military man trained to follow timings precisely, wound me up enormously. I was also still suffering from night terrors, which only got worse with the aggravation I suffered during the day.

I did move back down to the Portland area and rented an apartment for a short while when my employers wanted to try branching out to Oregon and I met a great girl who I had known in elementary school in Newport. It never occurred to me to tell her about what had happened to me in the military. It wasn't a 'Whoa! I can't tell her that!' It had just stopped being a conscious thought anymore because I had successfully sealed it in a vault in my mind. I was, however, ashamed to tell her that I had a daughter. In my head, I was no longer the hero; I was no longer the white picket fence guy. But women like honesty, right? They like vulnerability, don't they? So, eventually, I did pluck up the courage to tell her I had a daughter... and she never spoke to me again! So that informed me, 'Well, I definitely can't share that with anybody either, because I'm no longer the perfect marriage material, or even good marriage material,' so I hated myself even more and I would spend the next few years getting drunk and screwing women I didn't care about and not giving a shit and that left me even more hollow. I moved back to the Bay Area soon after that because selling wire and cable to constructors in Portland wasn't working out so well, but things didn't get any better.

I was sat, stationary, in grid-locked traffic on the San Mateo-Hayward Bridge one day, late for yet another appointment, my blood boiling, and I thought, 'I can't deal with this anymore.' I had watched CNBC that morning and listened to a stock market analyst and decided there and then I was going to be a stockbroker. I didn't know a bond from a 401 (k) retirement savings plan and I didn't have a college degree, but I knew that I could sell. I went for interviews in numerous places and Prudential Securities in Walnut Creek, CA, had a former military Colonel as their branch manager and he gave me a shot. He told me I had three months to pass the series 63, series 65 and series 7 exams needed to become a financial and life insurance advisor. If I failed any one of them I was done but, as I have said, I am pretty good at exams and I passed. I was not with Prudential Securities for long before I visited my mom who was then living in Albuquerque, New Mexico, and I was worried about the weed-head she was shacked up with so I applied for a job with Charles Schwab down there, interviewed, got the job and moved to Albuquerque to keep an eye on her. Outside of work, I was still trying to get my university degree so I attended the University of Phoenix in Albuquerque and did social sciences, which I enjoyed. The shame of it was that, even studying ancient cultures, philosophy and what shapes humans and why we do the things we do, I was no closer to realising the effect 'the incident' in Germany was having on my own behaviour.

It wasn't long before I got promoted and was asked to help out at the El Paso branch in Texas, and while there I won the Number

One outbound advisor award during a nationwide campaign but I didn't like El Paso much so I asked for a transfer to Seattle, where my dad was at the time. Business was good but my love life certainly was not. I don't remember dating anyone of note in Albuquerque, El Paso or Seattle but I was still in my going out and drinking and hating women mode, and the few buddies I met at the gyms were pretty flaky, so they didn't feature in my life much either. I hadn't been in Seattle for long before Edward Jones Investments came calling with the offer of a travelling advisor and I agreed. I made tons of money but, spending more than 300 days a year on the road, I had never felt more alone. That was when one of my old bosses at Charles Schwab reached out and asked if I wanted to help open a new branch in my hometown of Bend and I jumped at the chance to go home. I just didn't realise there was more violence and more heart-break waiting to stir the monster inside of me.

THE MONSTER INSIDE OF ME

CHAPTER TWELVE

It felt good to be home. Business was going well and I had more friends around me for the first time in years but, if I'm honest, that didn't mean that my life was anything but remarkably shallow. I was still very much in that mode of working and lifting weights all week, partying at the weekend and hooking up with girls whenever I could, without any kind of emotional commitment. I dated a couple of them for a few weeks at a time, maybe, but as soon as I felt like they were getting too close I dumped them. It was really not nice behaviour but the monster inside of me couldn't give a damn. The weight-lifting, I'm sure, was still that thing about making myself someone that no one would mess with. It's the same reason I have lots of tattoos. The hyper-vigilance is also why I always carry a gun and why, at the time, I was still getting into fights. A buddy and I were out in a dance club one night not too long after I had got back to Bend and this guy hit me on the back of the head because he was in a dust-up with someone else and because he had been thrown against me. Unaware of how he had come to hit me, I turned around and was like, 'Hey! What the fuck?' and the next thing I knew this idiot came after me, so I used a wrestling move to take him down. He was still trying to swing for me so I was holding him down when the bouncers came and ripped me off of him. I started to explain that I was just defending myself because, totally unprovoked, this guy had started to hit me, but they stood me up and held both my arms and, sure enough, my attacker took advantage and punched me right in the face.

Instead of letting me go, the bouncers insisted on me leaving. I told them, 'Look, I'm fine. It's the other guy who started all of this. Don't kick me out because that kid is going to be waiting for me out there...and I'm going to beat the shit out of him.' They ignored my protestations and kicked me out and, just as I had suggested, the kid was waiting to attack me again. I picked him up, slammed him down and elbowed him in the face, repeatedly. I have no idea what state he was in by the time I had finished because I started to hear police sirens so I just took off and got out of there. I know it was bullshit behaviour but my hyper-vigilance was at the top of the dial and when you add alcohol it's a real bad combination. So that was the brawling, but the promiscuity, I guess, was because I was terrified of falling in love. I didn't know why at the time - didn't know about my PTSD and the deep psychological scars the incident in Germany had left - but I felt sure that I couldn't handle any kind of meaningful relationship. Of course, plenty of people who don't have PTSD can behave like idiots: thoughtless and unconcerned about the consequences of their actions. So, was my behaviour just a manifestation of a natural selfishness in me? It's possible, but I'm sure that I wasn't like that before I was raped. I really don't believe that my behaviour was a reflection of the true me and I didn't like myself for it even as I was doing it. Nevertheless, my aversion to commitment continued. That was until I met Kelly.

She was auburn-haired, a good-looking gal, and we dated for a couple of months and we had some good times. Then, like the others, I dumped her, but his time things were different. Kelly wrote me an email like no-one had ever done before. She told me something like, 'Hey, I'm sad that you decided we didn't have a future together. I really liked you, we were good together and I thought we had a good chance,' and things like that and I hated myself more than ever for the way that I had treated her. Suddenly I was thrown out of my increasingly misogynistic comfort zone. With my inner turmoil prompting my frankly awful behaviour I could hardly claim to be a prize catch but Kelly clearly saw something in me, so maybe I had been too hasty in ending it with her, I thought. To be fair, while I was by no means perfect, there were plenty of reasons for me to be wary about Kelly too. She already had a son from a previous relationship, not to mention two other children she had given away for adoption at birth, but since I had a daughter – who I didn't get to see often - that was hardly a deal-breaker. Of more concern to me was the fact that she had had some issues with weed in the past and she had been indulged so much by her wealthy family throughout her life that I felt she had a tendency to behave like a spoiled princess. Even so, her letter really got to me and I told myself,' Well, maybe she is the one I should just marry. She comes from a good family. Her dad's a doctor, and I'm so great that we will be just fine!' Seriously, how deluded was I to think I didn't have my own shortcomings? But those were the thoughts going through my head. It was a terrible way to go into a marriage but my irrational, impulsive brain had made the decision for me, so we got back together. I think we dated a total of ten months and then we got married. I had asked her outright beforehand about her smoking weed and I told her I didn't like it because I had a relative who was a pot-head and a real piece of crap, and she swore up and down that she used to do drugs but didn't any more. I asked her about the drinking too and she was, like, 'Yeah, I might have a beer once in a while.' Well, it wasn't like I was a paragon of virtue, and ever since I was raped I had used alcohol as a crutch, stupidly self-medicating in the way that trauma victims do. So we got hitched. Besides, an ill-considered marriage was not the only mess that my fight-or-flight impulsiveness was getting me into.

Work-wise, I was doing so well at the time for Charles Schwab that my quarterly target for bringing in net new assets for the brokerage was $12 million, which was astronomical and four times higher than the next highest goal in the branch. There was no doubt that I was doing a good job but it's the nature of corporate business that they never let you rest on your laurels. They never ask you to do less, do they? They just keep wanting more and I was proud that I kept producing the goods, so when it came time for the quarterly review I was horrified to be rated 'Did not meet'. They told me that I hadn't met my target and I was furious. As far as I was concerned I had definitely met my $12 million goal but they told me I had only gained them $8 million in net new assets. They deducted $4 million from the total that I had calculated, taken from a single account that I had brought in, and they credited the acquisition of those assets to another guy, I'll call Jim. What had happened was that Jim had made a five minute cold call to a wealthy guy, and three or four months later the guy had come into the branch. He hadn't mentioned Jim at all - hadn't even remembered him, as far as I knew - and I talked to him for over two hours and got him to bring all of his accounts in and then invested them for him. OK, if the call from Jim had prompted the guy to come in, or if the guy had mentioned him, I could see that Jim would be due at least a partial claim on the business acquisition, but the bosses insisted it was entirely Jim's because he had made the original call. I told our regional VP that he should call the investor and ask him who he had the relationship with and why he had chosen to invest with us, because I knew it was down to me, but they said, 'No, we're not going to do that,' so the monster rose in me and I told them, 'Well, you're going to lose me then,' and I quit in a huff. That is the thing with my PTSD. I get triggered by unfairness and those atrocities that I see happen in the world, and I resent authority when it is wielded in an unfair way, which I'm sure is down to the trauma I suffered in the incident. It was, after all, authority that took all my power from me on that occasion and my promise to myself is that I'm never giving that up to someone again, right? So I quit a job that I was really good at, that was paying me $80,000 dollars a year, which was very good money at the time, rather than back down; rather than take the criticism and move forward in a positive way. And those irrational decisions have happened all through my life since I was 19. I won't say that I come unhinged, but I don't make sound decisions in those moments. I react in a way a reasonable person probably shouldn't.

The timing was horrible for Kelly and me. I had bought myself a small house not long before and then I moved Kelly in when we got married, plus she had a son to care for, remember, and she was a dog-groomer, so she wasn't making a ton of money. So I now had a mortgage, and dependents and responsibilities... and I had just decided to quit a really well-paying job in anger and go back to college to train as an attorney! Why an attorney? Well, at the time, Eliot Spitzer was the New York Attorney General who was going after all these corrupt people like Bernie Madoff and, while building on the work of the Securities and Exchange Commission (SEC), was having profound success, and his example inspired me to go back to school, finish my undergrad studies and get a law degree. I convinced myself that it was fine because I didn't have any other debts besides my mortgage but the fact was that I had just stopped my income and at the same time incurred more costs, because school isn't cheap. And then our son Calvin came along - a beautiful bundle of joy in my life, and very much wanted, but his arrival was not straightforward.

Kelly was perfectly composed when her waters broke. It was her fourth birth, remember. And me? I was just excited. I'm not a person to get in a panic in situations which other people might find stressful. I usually just get calm. I think, ironically, that my PTSD has perhaps played a part in that. My brain learned from traumatic experience that, in order to survive in moments of threat, I can't be hysterical. I have to be in control. I think, too, that that calmness is why I did OK on EMT calls during my time with Portland Fire Department, dealing with multiple car accidents, triaging casualties and the like, because I'm a pretty good decision-maker under the kind of pressure that others struggle with. I think it was also probably why, during my army career, I was a good soldier out in the field. It was mostly when I drank too much – to try to self-medicate my inner turmoil - that I lost control, and it has been when I have been triggered by perceived injustice or my fight-or-flight reflex has kicked in – rather than when I have simply been in high pressure situations – that I have made poor, impulsive decisions. So I was not feeling anything but thrilled at the prospect of seeing my new baby. All that was about to change, but there was no tough decision for me to make. It was all completely out of my hands and that only made it worse. The wonder and awe of that moment when my son was first delivered lasted just seconds before the mood in the delivery room darkened as our new infant remained ominously silent. Without saying a word to alarm us, the nurse quickly took Calvin aside and I found myself watching in horror as she was sternum-rubbing my brand new baby who was not breathing. I have never felt more scared in my life, or more helpless. There was literally nothing I, or Kelly could do as our child's life hung in the balance. It seemed like an eternity, but was probably a few seconds, before Calvin eventually gave a tiny scream, but then he was silent again as the nurse carried on rubbing his little chest. Less than a minute later he was whisked away to the neonatal intensive care unit (NICU) and we were all alone in the delivery room with no baby and all we could do was anxiously wait. Another nurse came in to explain that our baby was having trouble clearing the fluid in his lungs and that, though it was not exactly common, it was something that they dealt with on a semi-regular basis. They reassured us, but they could not stop us worrying and fearing the worst.

I can't tell you how long we waited, or how long the initial the emergency had lasted, or anything else that was happening beyond my recollection of feeling petrified the whole time. I think because of my PTSD, traumatic memories like that get buried; my brain just creates new neural pathways to diminish them. I know that as soon as Kelly was able to be moved they took us along to look in on our baby in the NICU, all wired up to monitors and with tubes down his little throat and once again I felt helpless. I think the initial fear subsided as they explained that he was safe and being looked after and I thank God that the nurses did such a good job, seeing the problem, recognising it and acting fast, but it still makes me cry thinking about that moment when we saw that he was not breathing and knowing that without that intervention he would have died. Calvin stayed in the NICU, being helped to breathe, for a week before he was considered well enough for us to take him home to our little house. It was a special moment as I carried my precious bundle into our home and at that moment I felt very close to Kelly and, after so many lonely years, I finally felt like I had found happiness. Colton, Kelly's young son, was also there for our return. I can't remember if my mom, or Kelly's family had been looking after him for the week while we were back and forth to the hospital – the whole drama had made my mind spin - but we seemed like a real family. Calvin remained a little asthmatic for a while, and struggled a bit as a baby, but he would soon grow stronger. Sadly, the same could not be said for Kelly and me.

CHAPTER THIRTEEN

It wasn't long before the rows started, and it was often due to my perception of Kelly's drug-use. She was constantly trying to hide her weed smoking from me, though you can always smell it – it's much worse than tobacco. There were other pressures too, for both of us. Calvin's traumatic arrival in the world had come at a cost. His seven-day stay in the NICU was ruinously expensive. The total bill, including what my insurance covered, was insane and even with the insurance I was still out of pocket $12,000 that we could ill afford. Without a steady income, I soon had to sell our house to pay the medical bills and we moved into rental accommodation. I never did finish my undergrad studies. I think I had probably got about a year of college in before this mini financial crisis hit and I came to my senses and it occurred to me, 'Oh, I've got to pay bills. I've got a family to take care of now.' A buddy who worked in staffing told me of the small, family-owned business that employed him and he said they were great to work for, so I had started as an account executive. Within three years or so I would go from account manager to branch manager in charge of five branches to VP of business development and I was making a good six figure salary, but by then the happy family vibe was definitely wearing thin and things were deteriorating with Kelly. God knows why – probably for Calvin's sake - but I hung in there, trying to make the marriage work. In fact, I not only hung in there, I also made another of those impulsive decisions. The owner of a Mexican restaurant we used to frequent had told me about this prime 20-acres site in Bend that had come up for sale – and they were much sought after – so, since we needed a house, I took what money was left from the sale of my previous house, took all the money I had gotten from Charles Schwab in stock options, plus any life savings I could scrape together, increased my mortgage, got a construction loan and bought the land to begin building my dream home. I project managed the build myself and used every lunchtime, plus hours after work, to make sure the job was done right and was on schedule so we would have the family home we wanted. Kelly chose some of the lighting, and did a good job, but other than that she had little involvement. Most of the decisions were left to me and I didn't really care that we weren't working on it together, sharing the dream. It was probably a huge warning sign at the time about the state of our marriage but, foolishly, I ignored it. Another of those missed red flags.

It was round about the time that construction of my $1.1 million dream home was being completed that my nightmare marriage was being reduced to rubble. Not long after we had moved into the new house I went away for the weekend on a small hunting trip with some buddies. It was not as full-on as some of the hunting trips I used to go on with my dad but we had fun and I got to unwind from some of the tensions that came with getting the house finished and arguing with Kelly about her drinking and pot-smoking. I felt good from the weekend and proud of the home I was coming home to that Sunday afternoon and, as I got off Highway 97, made my way through Bend and pulled my pick-up onto our driveway I was looking forward to seeing Calvin and also enjoying the luxury of the new house. My state of relaxation was shattered, though, when I saw my BMW X5 parked there with its rear end completely bashed in. It was totalled. My first thought was for Kelly and Calvin, who I thought must have been in the car when it was crunched, but as soon as I got in the house Kelly was strangely vague about what had happened and things started to seem suspicious. She told me she had been out with our day-care, Jackie, and that some random guy had smashed into her as she drove home, but she didn't sound concerned. She then said that the guy had crashed his own car further up Highway 20 a bit and had been arrested by the cops, but when I suggested calling the cops to find out what was happening with him, and asking them to press charges over the damage to my X5, she became defensive and insisted she was going to take care of it. When I pushed her further she was oddly protective of this 'random guy' she had never met, which made no sense at all. She said weird stuff like, 'He's obviously a drug addict and has had it tough so we should give him a break.' 'Give him a what?' It was ridiculous and my suspicions were growing. I spoke to Jackie and it didn't take long for me to figure out that she and Kelly had been out with this guy in a white trash bar not too far from our new home. I was pretty sure he had crashed into my car as he drove to our house and I had my suspicions why he was going there. I accused Kelly but she denied she had been having an affair. She still does to this day, but two married women – her and Jackie – going to a dive bar doesn't usually lead to good things. It wasn't too long afterwards that Jackie came clean and told me about the piece of crap who had totalled my car and she alleged that Kelly had be seeing him for some time. I confronted Kelly with Jackie's comments and she still flat out denied having an affair but, whatever she had been up to, our marriage had reached the end of the road and it was less than a couple of weeks before Kelly moved out and we both filed for divorce.

Just as our marriage fell apart, the subprime mortgage crisis and housing market crash of 2007/08 hit. The construction loan company wanted their money back and I could not get traditional financing because the housing market was going down the toilet. I tried to get a short sale and a doctor offered me something like $850,000, which was well below what the house was worth but which would have paid back the main $800,000 mortgage with $50,000 towards the second debt of $300,000, but the bank behind the construction loan refused to approve it. Well, this was right at the beginning of that housing market crash and the banks didn't know what was coming their way – though they certainly should have done - so I told them, 'Well, I'm going to have to file for bankruptcy and not only that but the house will sell on the County steps. It will come under foreclosure and you'll get nothing,' but they didn't give a crap. While I was having sleepless nights about my home being repossessed, Kelly was just fine, looked after by her rich daddy who had always bailed her out so that she never had to take responsibility for her chaotic life, and she was still happily screwing the low-life she had been cheating on me with. That didn't stop her texting me regularly, telling me she needed money, or diapers, or something, so I would go to Costco, or wherever, and buy diapers and I would show up at the dog grooming shop that I had built for her and she would have a huge, gross hickey on her neck, and if I dared to comment on it she would yell at me that it was none of my business. I wasn't sad that the marriage was ending. By then I viewed that as a good thing. What I hated was the constant fighting. I was trying to be a good guy, doing stuff that I really didn't need to do, fixing her air conditioning when it broke and sorting out other stuff for her. I mean, I hated her guts for what she had done, but I wasn't unhappy about helping because I reckoned it was for my son. Meanwhile, of course, she had taken my beloved pick-up truck for her own use and I had to watch the guy who had totalled my BMW X5 driving around in my pick-up with similar love bites to Kelly's on his neck, smoking cigarettes while my young son was in the back seat being poisoned by the smoke and it was all I could do not to murder someone at that point. I was literally going out of my mind. I had vowed after the incident in Germany that I would never again let someone take advantage of me and leave me feeling so humiliated, and here it was happening again.

I had been cheated on, I was losing my home and the person I cared most about – dearer to me than my own life – was sitting in the back of my pick-up being driven around by some junkie dude I didn't know, having the guy's foul cigarette smoke breathed all over him, and I was just supposed to swallow it. Everyone involved – including me – is very lucky that the monster inside of me didn't do what it wanted to do, because if it had I would still be in jail now.

CHAPTER FOURTEEN

Anyone who has been through a divorce will know how painful it is, and they will know that you get put through mandatory counselling for very good reason, and one of the first things that they tell you – once they have established that the marriage is beyond salvation – is 'Do not date someone again for a minimum of a year'. Well they certainly told me that and it is really, really good advice but, of course, with my impulsive PTSD brain I completely ignored it because I was going through emotional hell, rattling around on my own in my luxurious 3,000 sq ft custom-built home, going nuts. The house was beautiful and I had picked just about every fixture and fitting in the place, so there was nothing for me not to like. Also, like everyone else in my position at that time, I had stopped paying the mortgage and was just waiting for the bank to foreclose, which was not happening quickly, so I was living there for free. But that was of no comfort whatsoever as I knew I was inevitably going to lose it and be left with virtually nothing. There were other outgoings, of course. I couldn't file a Chapter Seven bankruptcy because I was earning too much so I had to file a Chapter Thirteen, which was a repayment programme. At least I had my work to keep me occupied during the day but in the evening, back at home, I was on my own, lonely as hell in my gilded cage with only painful memories to torment me. I couldn't sleep at night and I would lie there sweating profusely, partly because of the anxiety over my future but also - less obviously to me - because of the demons of my past. My night terrors, which had dogged me ever since the incident in Germany, were worse than ever; vivid and inescapable. I had no peace, no rest, and the walls just seemed to close in around me. The break-up of my marriage and the imminent loss of my home were just the perfect storm of shit and so, predictably, I tried to drown my sorrows.

Evenings would find me frequenting El Caporal, the Mexican bar and restaurant whose owner was my neighbour since he had recommended the plot of land next to his on which I had built my doomed dream home. Sometimes I would see him there. More often I would sit and chat to Julieta, the Mexican bar tender, and why not? She was absolutely gorgeous. I mean drop-dead beautiful. Now, I was by then in my late 30s while she was in her late 20s – so at least 11 years younger than me. With her looks she could have had any man she wanted, but she seemed to have set her sights on me. Why? I would love to believe it was my good looks and charm but, more realistically, it was because she was an illegal alien with a young son to support and I was obviously a soft target. So she invited me out for beers and the next thing I know I'm in a sexual relationship with her. Once again in my life I was ignoring all kinds of red flags, but in my blinkered view it was all pretty fantastic, and I'll admit I was thinking with what was between my legs rather than what was between my ears. She was not only super good looking but she would do everything a man wanted – certainly everything an emotionally bruised and lovesick man like me craved. She would wash my feet, give me massages and do all the sexual stuff I could dream of and so, of course, I was pretty quickly hooked in. At least it meant I had some comfort and an ally, rather than just an empty, doomed house and increasing levels of despair as the arguments with Kelly got worse the more we tried to settle our finances, and custody of Calvin. The divorce process is one that I would not wish on my worst enemy. The courts in the US are very one-sided towards the mother, and I know that there is good precedent for that, but good men really get beat up by the system. If you are good dad; if you want to be a good dad and things to be fair, it's a huge uphill battle. Over the years I have got a lot of friends who have been alienated by their children through the actions of their ex-wives, and the list of that happening to men is long in the US. There is also a very long list of men who are complete crap heads, of course, which is where it gets hard to defend men as a whole. It's a really tough one to work out and it makes it incredibly difficult for everyone involved, and it was certainly getting to me. And it wasn't just Calvin. There was Kelly's son Colton, too, whose father had never really been part of his life. He had been growing up as part of our family and he was attached to me and I was attached to him and I tried to have him remain in my life, but Kelly was being so erratic. On one of the few occasions when my own father took an interest in my life he told me I would have to give up on that hope because, as he pointed out, Kelly's family was rich and she only had to throw a tantrum – and she did regularly – and they would pay for an attorney for her and I did not have that kind of money to be going to court all the time with an attorney of my own. And of course he was right and they soon enough did get her an attorney.

The sad thing is that, originally, Kelly and I had sat down with a yellow pad of paper and we'd agreed I would give her $500 a month, and I would spend half of the time with Calvin, and that seemed reasonable to me, especially with the money I was making. But then her mother told her, 'Well you need to get an attorney,' and it all went to hell from there. I still said it was fine if the attorney wrote up what we had agreed, and made it a legal agreement. I made it clear I would not sign off on anything that was significantly different to what we had agreed, but every time that Kelly would go to her attorney and tell her to write it up the way we had agreed, the attorney would change something – usually just one thing - significantly in Kelly's favour and it happened something like ten or 12 times. After it had happened the first few times I said I would not sign it off and that I was fine just going to court and doing whatever the judge decided, because that was my last line of defence, but this attorney kept tweaking and tweaking and tweaking over and over again and I finally got mad at Kelly and I told her, 'You and your mother are idiots. This woman is milking you for money. You and I agree on what the agreement should look like, and I keep giving more concessions - a little bit every time - and then she'll come back and something else won't be what you and I agreed to. I bet every time you visit that woman it costs you a couple of grand, and I don't care, but I'm not signing off on what that attorney is writing if it doesn't come back the way we agreed and we can just go to court.' I also threatened that I would get a forensic accountant to look at Kelly's tax returns. I think that, between that and her finally realising that the attorney was indeed milking her, she finally got pissed at the attorney and demanded that she just write up the agreement the way she told her to. I won't say that the final agreement was fair to me – I would end up paying almost $1,000 a month for 15 years or so, even when my finances were a lot worse than when we had made the agreement, and I could have gone back to court and got my payments significantly reduced, but I just wanted peace.

It took a year of conflict to get the divorce decree finalised and every months it was making me more depressed, like death by a thousand cuts. At least I had the company of Julieta, and she was sleeping at my place, which suddenly didn't feel so empty, but she was crying in my bed about being deported with her son so I said, 'Look, this is against my better judgement ...' - as if I had shown much good judgement for the previous 19 years - '... but I will marry you so you can't be deported, but you have to promise me that in a year or two we can have an actual real wedding that makes sense. Before that, I have got to get this house sorted and I have got to get my job sorted.' I loved my work with Staffing Services but they needed me to travel and I just couldn't while I was mentally and emotionally still going through hell with Kelly and trying to have time for shared care of Calvin. So I left Staffing Services and I got recruited by a new staffing firm called BBSI and I had a $100,000 salary, plus bonuses, and things like that, and I was still in my dream house for the time being, so I married Julieta when the divorce was finalised and guess what! The massages stopped and the sexual favours stopped and she became a completely different person, drinking a ton, slapping me, slapping her son, and calling the cops on ME. I never laid a finger on her but I had the sheriff out at my house several times after she called 911 making completely bogus allegations. She would kick in doors, smash crockery and hurl abuse at me. She was also cheating on me with other men, I would later learn. Her violent behaviour alone was absolutely intolerable, so I kicked her out, and that should have been that but I still let her talk me into joint counselling and brought her back into my life. More fool me, eh? There was one time when we had gone to dinner with my friends Mike and Emily - and her son and my boy Calvin were with us - and Julieta apparently did not like the way I had been looking at Emily, which was crazy. Mike and Emily, who I had met at Crossfit, had been friends from long before I met Julieta and Mike was living with me when they first got together so they were both just really good buddies, but as we were driving home from dinner Julieta started screaming at me, ignoring the fact that the kids were in the back seat having to listen to it. She wound up taking the left-overs that we had brought away from the meal and throwing them in my face as I was trying to drive. Then, as we pulled up outside where she was living, in order for me to drop her off, she reached into a bag of groceries in the back, grabbed a full plastic gallon carton of milk and smacked me in the face with it so hard that I ended up with a huge black eye. By this time I had had enough and, having parked my Ford Excursion, I grabbed the milk carton and I chased her out of the car, grabbed her, held the carton above her head and said, 'If you ever do anything like that to me again I will kill you.' I let her go but she was still chasing me and swinging at me, so I gently got her son out of the back of the SUV and closed all the doors. I put him down near their front door and went to get back in the Excursion but she would not let me get back in, hitting and kicking me. I pushed her back far enough, I thought, to race back to the car but as I got in and went to close the door her hand got trapped as she grabbed for me once more. I opened the door enough for her to pull her hand free then shut it again, locked it and slowly drove away. Yet again she called the cops but when they came to see me I only had to show them my black eye - and invite them to talk to Calvin who had seen the whole thing - and they agreed that my story tallied with what she had said, minus a few things that she had left out and a few bogus allegations that she had added, and they weren't interested in taking it further. There was no end to the lies Julieta told.

That milk carton episode was the final straw and the end of the relationship as far as I was concerned and I filed for divorce, but as she continued to push for asylum and a green card she went on to claim to the local Catholic church that we had split because I was an abusive husband, addicted to porn, and she sent me copies of the screen shots of supposed porn sites on my phone that she had sent to the church as 'proof'. They were, in fact, free online gambling sites that I had looked at a couple of times because I am not and never have been addicted to porn. She just made up whatever she wanted to make up to get what she wanted and used whoever she needed to, and I had been too blind to see it when she first came on to me. So now I was the poor sap dealing with abusive calls from Julieta while I also still had Kelly screaming at me on the phone or whenever I had to see her face to face. It was unrelenting and it was tearing me apart. My attempts to escape the misery of my first marriage break-up, and the imminent seizure of my home, had only led me to more misery and I was drowning in it. When I was not being yelled at by one or both of them I was alone in my house with the walls and all my problems closing in on me and it was torture. As if the betrayal by not just one but two wives in quick succession, and the imminent loss of everything I had ever worked for was not enough to explain the black mood I had descended into, I was unaware that my undiagnosed PTSD from my long-buried rape was also driving me down into a deep depression, punctuated by crippling moments of despair during the day and brutal night terrors. I had no will left to live. I hated everything about living and I wanted so badly for it all to stop. When I thought about those I would leave behind – Calvin, my parents, my siblings and friends – I truly believed that they would be better off without me. In my head I had failed to be the man I had always hoped I would be and I hated failure. I had let everyone down and I had let myself down, so what was the point in carrying on?

It must have been on a weekend when I decided to bring it all to an end because I was still at home, alone, at 9am or 10am in the morning after another broken night of fitful sleep, cold sweats, anxiety attacks and terrifying nightmares. I was exhausted. Overwhelmed. I didn't know where to turn next or even that I wanted to. That's when I told myself 'I'm going to take a shower and I'm going to blow my head off.' I didn't feel at that moment that anyone would miss me. Certainly neither Kelly nor Julieta would, that was for sure. Of course I loved my parents, because they had always done the best they could for me, but I wasn't thinking about them. I wasn't even thinking about Calvin. It was purely about me – not anyone else - and about ending my agony.

My thoughts were so far away from what my death would mean for those who loved me that my only reasoning was that if I killed myself in the shower it would be easier for anyone who found me to clean up the mess! The decision to end my life wasn't a hard one. I was tearful that it had come to this but I was devoid of any energy and too emotionally numb to cry as I stripped off, stepped into the shower and put my pistol within easy reach. I turned on the faucet and sat down in the shower tray. I took a moment to look around me at what would be the last thing I would ever see. I had spent so much time picking out the bathroom suite, choosing the faucets and every other fitting in that room and now it all felt utterly meaningless. The water poured down on me like the torrents of rainfall I had been used to when I was a kid in Newport; like the tepid cascade the army had used to try to cool me down when I collapsed in my first week of basic training, but those relatively benign memories were a long way in the distant past and didn't even touch my consciousness as I reached for my gun and put it in my mouth, angled upwards towards my brain. 'One firm squeeze and it will all be over,' I told myself over and over again as I flicked off the safety catch and rested my finger on the trigger, but I couldn't pull it, and I couldn't pull it, and I couldn't pull it. I took the gun out of my mouth, then tried again a few moments later and this dance with death was repeated countless times. I don't know how long I was sat there but the hot water had soon turned lukewarm, then cold, then freezing, still pouring down on me, and each time I failed to pull the trigger I berated myself. 'You're a sissy and a coward! Just be a man and pull the fucking trigger!' I told myself until I got to the point where I was definitely going to do it, like when you're preparing to jump off a high ledge into the sea or a river far below and you delay and delay until the moment you tell yourself 'Well, fuck it, I'm going to jump!' and you jump, and I had finally reached that moment. My hand...my whole body was shaking from the cold but I slowly put the gun back in my mouth and began squeezing the trigger. It's my belief that at that moment it was God who flashed a vision of Calvin's face in my brain. I hadn't even thought about him, and the effect it would have on him, when I chose to end my life but now it was all I could see, like a bolt of lightning, and I put the gun down for the last time. The only thing that had saved my life was the thought of my little boy and I thank God that I didn't pull the trigger.

CHAPTER FIFTEEN

Testimony of US Army female veteran 'B' – twice raped in the military.

I was a female soldier in the U.S. Army between 1987 and 1991. I was a transportation specialist and my first duty station was in Kaiserslautern, Germany. At nineteen years old it was my first time away from home. A fellow soldier invited me to a Christmas party at his apartment off base along with several others. He worked at headquarters and was close to all the sergeants and commander. He was a specialist (E-4) while I was a private (E-2). There was alcohol involved, but everyone was having fun. He attacked me in the kitchen and raped me while I was heading to the bathroom. No one could hear my muffled screams; he had his forearm over my face and everybody else was passed out. He threatened to report my 'misconduct' to the commander, even though I hadn't done anything wrong. He also claimed no one would believe me. He said I was just a typical slut looking for a good time, so he had 'obliged'. Being new to the unit I felt they wouldn't believe me, a mere private, and everyone told me what a great guy he was. I knew I'd end up being humiliated and then I still had to serve another year and a half with these same people. So, I kept my mouth shut, kept my head down and soldiered on.

Towards the end of my service I spent nine months in Saudi Arabia during the First Gulf War in a specialty unit of fifteen transportation specialists, and I was the only female. My sergeant was very charming and charismatic, everyone adored him. I looked up to him for guidance and he seemed ok. After our deployment we arrived back in the United States to Ft. Lewis, Washington. I was out-processing because my end of time in service was overdue since they'd involuntarily extended my time due to the war. I'd survived stepping on a land mine and the nightly bombings and was excited just to be alive and going home. I was invited to a going-away party for our detachment, or at least that's what my sergeant told me. I arrived at his room because he had said we were all to meet there, then go out for dinner and drinks. When I entered the room he handed me a cocktail, then another. I hadn't eaten so it seemed to go straight to my head. I told him I'd wait downstairs; that I needed some air. He blocked me from leaving the room, locked the door and threw me down on the bed and raped me. I fought, but the harder I fought the more he made it hurt. Afterwards he told me not to tell anyone or I wouldn't be able to out-process and go home. He said they'd never believe me over him and, at that point, I believed him because I was traumatized and scared. I kept my mouth shut again and left the military. I should have been feeling proud of my service and looking forward to new chapters in my life but instead I was left feeling terrible.

I kept my war trauma and MSTs a secret for 30 years. I buried them deep and avoided remembering them at all cost. I was a registered nurse, but my symptoms of PTSD became so severe that I had to retire. I was unable to work due to flashbacks, nightmares, memory loss and anger. I hated myself and everyone around me. I isolated myself and convinced myself I deserved whatever I was suffering; that I had brought it on myself; that I shouldn't have been drinking; that I should've known better. I never wanted to admit it happened because I was a soldier yet I was too weak to save myself and fight off my attackers. I became suicidal and eventually had to go to a Women's Trauma Recovery Program through the VA. If I hadn't gone to that program, I wouldn't be here today. MST must be stopped. The military must be held accountable. This can't continue to happen. Too many of us have already suffered.

CHAPTER SIXTEEN

My suicide attempt had frightened the hell out of me and I knew that I needed to get help otherwise I was likely to try again and the next time I might just succeed, leaving Calvin without a dad. It didn't help that two or three people who were well known in our smallish community had lost everything, having invested heavily in real estate, and had killed themselves, and I had arguably got more reason to feel my life was pointless. My issues went far beyond simply losing property or money. The mental anguish of two broken relationships cannot be overstated and underlying it all was the PTSD I didn't know I was suffering with, which already made me feel worthless. I wish I could have been calmer about all the things that were pushing me into the abyss, and not let that stuff get to me, but I couldn't, so I started looking online for a psychiatrist. I didn't know what I was looking for; what areas of expertise they should have; what specialisation – if any – would be best to help me. I just plumped for one of the first I came across and arranged to see her. I turned up for our appointment and I explained that I had attempted suicide and that I thought I probably needed help and she listened, then prescribed me some pills and basically said I seemed OK but that the medicine would help me. To be honest, it felt to me that she was pretty dismissive. She was working in an area popular with wealthy Californian transplants so I guess she happily counted a few of them among her clients. It must have been clear to her that I wasn't rich like them so it felt like she couldn't be bothered to establish a rapport as a basis for a long-term working relationship because having me as a client wasn't going to pay her too many dividends. She certainly didn't ask me about my distant past or get even close to working out why I might have been suicidal. I had long since buried my rape in my subconscious, so it wasn't likely that she would have unearthed that very easily. Hell, I wasn't even aware of that myself, but she didn't really delve into my dire personal circumstances at all, as far as I can recall. Maybe it was my own fault. When you're younger you still think you're a force, right, and I'm sure I probably just went in there and downplayed everything, but I definitely told her I had tried to kill myself and you'd think that that might make a psychiatrist want to dig a little bit deeper, wouldn't you? But she was like, 'You seem fine. Take these, OK?' So I did, at first. I took the anti-depressants and I hated the way they made me feel and I hated what they did to my body, so I stopped taking them after just a couple of weeks. Mercifully, I found some help from an unexpected source.

Much as I had decided that my marriage to Julieta was over, and the divorce was going through, she still persuaded me to do some couples therapy. She had found this guy through a friend of hers and I agreed to meet him with her. Perhaps it was more evidence of my PTSD, my feeling of worthlessness and my constant desire to please people, which inevitably led to feelings of failure if I didn't make them happy. The dude that Julieta insisted we see wasn't a licensed therapist in any way, shape or form. I seem to remember he called himself a 'sifu mystic' but he was OK and I liked him straight away. He's a good guy and he agreed to do some counselling for the two of us. The interesting thing was that we weren't many sessions in before Julieta stormed out saying that he was taking sides with me – which he wasn't – and she refused to go back. I was the one trying to make changes and do things and be agreeable and she wasn't and even though she had found this guy and persuaded me to see him, she stopped going because she was just a train wreck. I continued for a little while on my own but it wasn't too many sessions after that that he just grabbed me by the shoulders, looked me in the eye and told me, 'It's not you Ron. You're a good person; a good human,' and him saying that to me seemed to lift a massive weight off my shoulders and at that point I thought, 'Yeah, I am.' You know, I know my core. I know I can be passionate, a little much, and my thinking is often too black and white, and I now know that that is caused by my PTSD, but I felt at the time that I had always been a good person at heart. The occasional times when the monster had been aroused within me were out of character and I'm not and never have been malicious. I don't do things maliciously, and so it felt like tonnes had been lifted off me and that's the moment I knew Julieta and I were finished. I met up with her for a coffee after that and I sat her down and I told her, 'Look, I'm done. Forever. That's it. Just lose my number because you're weird, you've taken advantage of me and I don't ever want to have contact with you, ever again,' And that hurt because, like Colton, her son Alan was a little older than Calvin but I had gotten to care for him and not seeing her would mean not seeing him again. After I divorced her she wound up seducing the CEO of a publicly-traded company and cajoling him into making her his bookkeeper. They would take glorious trips to Las Vegas and spend crazy amounts of the company's money, all of which she would hide in the accounts. Unsurprisingly, when the fraud came to light and they were both federally indicted, she turned on him and took a plea and he is probably still in jail. But that was in the future.

In the present, I was still taking a financial hit because of my Chapter Thirteen bankruptcy so I concocted a plan to lose my job and to fail to find another job of equal value for six months or more. That would mean I could move to a Chapter Seven and stop the repayments to my creditors. I knew it would mean that the banks, who don't care about divorce decrees, would then go after Kelly and I knew that her father wasn't going to write her a check for $500,000 so she too would have to file for bankruptcy.

I can't say that that bothered me too much, either, because she was swanning around scot-free, thinking she had gotten away with the house debt and all those things that I was lumbered with. I had by then left Staffing Services and had been recruited by BBSI, which came with bonuses on top of the $100,000 salary. It was a good job, so deliberately getting myself fired was not the greatest idea ever but I was not the most mentally stable guy at the time. It was also not so easy to do, because I had so many friends and work connections and they kept bringing me business. Nevertheless, I would do as little work as possible. I would sit in my office and just take a nap and I didn't give a crap. I told myself at the time that it was all part of a plan to change my bankruptcy status and to get back at Kelly, but I suspect that any psychiatrist looking at my lethargy, my nap-taking and my total disconnect from any responsibility might see classic signs of depression instead. Not caring about my future, or what happened to me, was also a common symptom of PTSD, but eventually BBSI did let me go and that in itself did actually help my mental state. With time on my hands, I got seriously into Crossfit and did a bunch of yoga and I did start to feel fairly decent about myself. Being out of a relationship also seemed to take some pressure off of me. I not only didn't have a steady relationship, I didn't get remotely close to anybody at that time, and I didn't need to. I had Calvin to look after whenever it was my turn to do so, and I looked forward to that so much.

My dream house did indeed sell at public auction, as I had predicted, and it went for a fraction of what it was worth. When I was finally able to get a new house of my own I bought it from my surrogate sister Dani and it was tiny – less than 1,000 sq ft – with just two bedrooms, and I was sleeping in bunk beds with my son in one of them and me in the other while I had my mom living in the other room because she was going through a tough time herself and needed a place to stay, so there was not a lot of romance going on! I was certainly not bringing ladies home to that, and I was happy. I had no one I was desperately trying to please and no one to make me feel I was failing abysmally if I didn't achieve that one small thing. When the Chapter Thirteen bankruptcy finally went to a Chapter Seven and I was able to look for work again, I took a job in car sales for a little while because I had always wanted to do that. I wondered what it would be like and I thought I might be good at it. As it happened, it was exactly what you might think it was – crazy hours and very cut-throat, so that quenched that particular desire and while I was still doing that job I asked my buddy Dan, who worked for a motorcycle parts distributor, 'Are there any jobs where you're working at Parts Unlimited?' and he said, 'Yeah, they're looking for my boss right now,' so, on a whim, I sent my résumé in and I interviewed with the national sales manager and I wound up getting the job. It meant I started travelling a lot, visiting the reps I was responsible for, riding with them as they distributed parts to different motorcycle dealerships, evaluating them and trying to help them improve, but I'd usually have a home week now and again and I would have Calvin then, and I would always have him on the weekends because Kelly wanted to go off partying. If I went to play golf he went with me; if I did Crossfit he'd come to the gym with me; and if I had a barbeque or went to a barbeque he went with me. The pressures that had been building up before I tried to take my own life seemed to be behind me, at least for the time being. I was more relaxed than I had been for years. My mental health was much better and some of the happiest times of my life, that I can remember, were going to sleep in my bunk, listening to the gentle breathing of my seven-year-old son in the bunk above me, knowing that he was safe and peacefully asleep and that I was there to care for him.

And then, out of the blue, I ended up in jail.

CHAPTER SEVENTEEN

The kid sharing the cell with me was asleep when the warder came around with our meals. In fact, he had been asleep for almost the whole time I had been in there, probably because he was a junkie who had been high for days straight before they threw his ass in jail. I gave him a nudge, then a harder nudge when he wouldn't wake up initially. It wasn't the first time I had had to wake him to eat but at least I wasn't locked behind bars with some violent psychopath ranting and raving. On that score I could have counted myself lucky, but I didn't feel lucky at all. I felt totally pissed at the injustice of it all. There had been plenty of times when I probably should have been put in jail – times when, though I didn't realise it, my PTSD, combined with drink, had led me to do things I later bitterly regretted. But this wasn't one of those occasions. The monster inside of me had barely stirred. So how had I landed in this mess? My job at the time was really relaxed, I had no ongoing romance to send my stress levels soaring, I was loving the time I got to spend with now eight-year-old Calvin and my physical fitness was doing wonders for my emotional fitness, so the latest blip in my life came right out of the blue. It certainly didn't seem to have anything to do with my mental state. Yes, my undiagnosed PTSD may have played a part, in that my fight-or-flight reflex was triggered by me witnessing an injustice, but I never felt like I was out of control.

I guess it was the protector in me that was awoken because it was hearing the commotion of someone else having a hard time that had drawn me into a situation that I had played no part in starting. I had been to CrossFit, working on my fitness, and afterwards went out with a group of people from the gym. I didn't even drink that much but the girls in our group wanted to go into this one particular bar. It just happened to have a reputation for trouble caused by their over-aggressive bouncers, but the girls were adamant so that's where we went. We had been there a while and I was just having a beer, chatting to some people, when there was the noise of shouting outside, involving some of our party, and I went outside just in time to see my buddy's wife get slapped to the ground by one of the bouncers. As I said, I had not had much to drink but there's something about bullies that really pushes my buttons and I was thinking, 'Not on my watch!' I was not about to let the attack on a woman go unchallenged so I went to remonstrate with the bouncer. Angry words were spoken, by me and by him, but there had been no aggression on my part before, without warning, I was attacked by one of the other bouncers. I'm talking about a big 275 lbs weightlifting dude who took it into his head to lay into me. It took me by surprise but I quickly recovered. I never threw a punch, but I took him down with a wrestling throw and then I got up and I walked away. The meathead – who I would later discover got fired from another job for skipping work and pretending to be getting cancer treatment - clearly didn't take kindly to being so easily grounded, and made to look weak, because he came round from behind a group of people who had gathered near the bar and he rushed me again. That's when I double-legged him and slammed him to the ground – or what I thought would be the ground. In fact, we had clearly moved closer to the bar and closer to the front window than I realised, and we both went through the plate glass. It was never what I planned to do but I was wrestling with a monster and things don't always go the way you plan. So the bottom of the window shattered and the top half came crashing down on both of us like a guillotine, but because I was on top of the meathead, effectively protecting him, it sliced the back of my head, causing a cut that would need 30 staples. At that point the other bouncers all descended on me at once, kicking and hitting me. I got myself to my feet and as the blood poured down me the guy who had first attacked me said, 'I hope you die. I've got camera footage of all of this,' and I said, 'Good. I'm glad you've got footage because it will show I didn't throw a punch. I was just defending myself when I took you down and you didn't like it.' Pretty soon the police turned up and I told them exactly what had happened. I had loads of witnesses and even the guy who had called 911 agreed, 'Yeah, he wasn't the aggressor, he was trying to get away from the dude,' but the cops didn't care. As far as they were concerned it was a bar brawl so I must be drunk and I must have started something, and they charged me with a felony offence and I told them, 'Just get the video evidence and you will see I was not to blame.' Well, on the Monday morning I got myself an attorney and he went to get the video evidence from the bar and, of course, they had deleted it so it was just my word against the bouncer's. By the time it got to court I was already out of pocket $10,000 for legal fees and the attorney told me it would cost another $10,000 to contest the case, which I could not afford, so I did an Alford plea, which is like pleading guilty without admitting guilt, on the understanding that the district attorney would knock the charge down to a misdemeanour – 'criminal mischief', or something like that - and I would not face any jail time. I also agreed to pay for the window. We made the point to the judge that the bar had deleted the video evidence because they knew it would support my argument, but the judge was only interested in what the police said and the police had no interest in getting to the truth, so the judge said, 'You're 45 and you shouldn't be involved in these things. I'm going to put you three days in county jail.' It was totally against what had been agreed with the district attorney but the judge wanted to flex his muscles and there was nothing I could do about it. I took a day's vacation so that Parts Unlimited did not need to know why I was really absent from work, and I spent three days in the slammer. You know, I did do a lie-detector test to try to support my case but we didn't mention it in court because I failed it. I don't know how those things work but I'm pretty certain I failed it because I was so worked up about the injustice of it all. I wasn't lying. I told the truth about what had happened but I know I do get wound up and when you're sitting on decades of hyper-vigilance built up because of undiagnosed PTSD, that can't be good for a lie detector test, I suspect. Anyway, I still seethe about the injustice of me being put in the slammer but the jail time was easy enough. I was lucky to have taken a couple of books with me so I just read those and bided my time.

If that was a red flag that the cauldron of emotions within me was still bubbling, then once again I missed it. As far as I was concerned, apart from that isolated incident, my mental health was good and work with Parts Unlimited was not putting me under any undue pressure. The only reason I left that job was because they fired my boss - the guy who had brought me in - and replaced him with a guy I didn't really like, respect or admire. At the same time the owner of TecMate was trying to recruit me so I decided to join them. It meant I was responsible for all of North America, including Canada, for my particular role at TecMate. The days spent travelling were similar to my previous job. I was just travelling further. I still had plenty of time with Calvin and,

just days before my 50th birthday, I met a new girl – Justine – who had recently been divorced. Things were great between us right

from the off, but when I had a big 50th birthday with friends at one of my favourite restaurants I didn't invite her along because I didn't want to rush things, or put her under pressure at a big gathering. Nevertheless, things got serious between us pretty quickly after that and, much as I struggled with relationships, it was great to have that feminine company and to share a woman's bed once more, and she was an incredible gal and that, indirectly, led to a bit of an issue at my work that would end up triggering me and stirring the monster again. You see, Justine had sent me some risqué photos – of her breast, as I recall – and I screwed up big time and put them into the wrong drop box and they were seen by a young guy, John, who worked out of our headquarters in Canada and who I had interviewed and approved for his job. As soon as I realised what had happened I told John, 'Oh God, I'm so sorry. I apologise. Please delete them,' and as far as I know, he did and he never mentioned it to my boss. Perhaps the smart thing would have been for me to mention it to my boss myself, accept the blame, apologise profusely and promise him it would not happen again, but I had spoken mano a mano with John and I just expected that to be an end to the matter, which it seemed to be. I quickly put it to the back of my mind but sometime later we were at one of our big annual trade shows in Madison, Wisconsin, and John got obscenely drunk. I won't say that I wasn't slightly intoxicated too, because I had had some drinks, but I certainly wasn't drunk, and he was. He was making an ass out of himself in the Hilton bar where all of our manufacturers' representatives - guys whose companies we distributed to - liked to hang out and it was not good for business to be making an ass of yourself there, so I pulled him to one side and said, 'Hey, John, you should probably head up to your room. You're pretty sauced up.' It was meant well but probably not said too sensitively. My priority was that he would not screw up any of our business relationships, but he took offence. He started telling me how I was lucky to have a job and that he could get me fired, and he was going on about those photographs from months earlier that I had forgotten all about. All at once I was feeling hostility, injustice and a moment that required fight or flight and that triggered me. I said, 'Are you threatening my job?' and he kept going on and on and he was right up in my face so I just left-hooked him in the throat and knocked him down. I didn't follow up. I didn't jump on him. I didn't do anything else, but it was certainly something that I should not have done – another impulsive reaction to my hyper-vigilant state. I did meet up with him later and apologised and I thought we had worked it out but of course it got back to the boss, because it happened where it happened, and he had a talk with me about it and I explained the scenario, but it was kind of the beginning of the end for me with Tecmate. I had already started not doing things exactly the way he wanted things done and he wound up letting me go, and it was a symptom of how my life was starting to spiral down once more.

CHAPTER EIGHTEEN

It was not just the end for me at TecMate but it kind of ruined my name in the motorcycle industry too and, in hindsight, it was probably an end to the healthy head space I had gotten to. At least things were pretty good between Justine and me, though alcohol was playing rather too big a part in our lives. We were both drinking too much which, as I now know, was not good in combination with the PTSD I didn't realise I had. We had fun when we were drinking, but we also had rows and once again I was always ready for a fight. Instead of simply apologising for anything that I had done to make her unhappy, explaining that it was never my intention and leaving her to process her own thoughts, I would always get defensive; taking on her emotions as well as my own; draining my capacity to cope. Then I would get argumentative and end up going loony tunes. We would always make up afterwards but it was starting to take its toll and the pressures on me were slowly ratcheting up once more. Workwise, I decided to go back to staffing and I reached a deal with a guy, Michael, who had experience in a big family staffing business and who wanted to set up his own company in Portland and he agreed we would split the business 60/40. We shook hands on it and I came up with a name for the business and all of the content for the website and Justine made a website virtually for free. Within a year, having started with a small business loan – so, effectively $150,000 in debt – we were $200,000 to the plus and I had brought in every single account but I was only getting the $48,000 start-up salary I had agreed to and I was still waiting for our ownership agreement to be formalized. In the meantime, I was paying for a rental apartment in Portland,

and travelling backwards and forwards to see Justine in Bend, and I had Calvin to worry about, so the stresses were definitely growing without me necessarily realising it. I had gone in three different times, over an eight month period, and asked Michael, 'Hey, when are we going to legalize and make permanent this partnership?' and he kept dragging his feet and dragging his feet and dragging his feet until, eventually, Justine wondered if he might be trying to screw me over. So I finally forced a bonus of around $25,000 out of him and I quit to start up my own business – Big Foot Staffing.

A salary of $48,000 did not go far on the West Coast, so that was all pretty much used up just living, and I only had the $25,000 to get my company up and running. The income from the business did come in quite quickly once we got started, because I didn't have any kind of 'no compete' clause with Michael and I had brought all my clients over with me, but for the first four or five, maybe six months I really wasn't making anything. I was borrowing money from my sister just to buy gas and there were times when I had some panic attacks which were red flag warnings that I was heading to a dark place once more. At the same time, the Covid-19 pandemic hit and, when it did, Portland was a particularly bad place to be. There were homeless people all over the city, there were riots and Portland was beyond a shit show. I hated being there and I hated my son being there, because when the restrictions were imposed he stayed with me and did his home schooling from there. It didn't feel much better when the restrictions were lifted so I just didn't want to be there. Portland definitely was not the place for me. Maybe I was subconsciously aware of how my mental health was suffering because around about that time it occurred to go to see a doctor for a check-up but not for anything in particular. I was just aware that I hadn't seen a doctor in a long time and I thought it made sense to get a physical, or something like that, and one of my friends said, 'Well, you're a veteran, you should go to the VA. You're poor right now, and being a veteran entitles you to some benefits, so why not go and see if they can help you?' I don't know why I hadn't considered the VA before. Did I have a jaundiced view because of how I felt I had been treated in the military, or had I heard too many stories of people being unhappy with the VA? I don't think it was either. I think I had just never felt like I needed their help before, but now, wanting to see a doctor, I definitely did need their help. So I went to the clinic in Bend to enquire and the guy I saw at reception told me why my lack of funds made me eligible for treatment, so I had a check-up and physically I was fine, and that was all they checked on because I gave them no reason to think my mental state was in any way fragile. Apart from anything else, that would have felt like showing weakness and, remember, ever since the incident in Germany I had been determined not to show weakness again. My financial situation began to improve quickly after that as the business took off, but life in Portland wasn't getting any better and it wasn't long before I was looking to sell my business and get out of it. I was on a vacation in Mexico with Justine when a friend, Jeremy, contacted me, expressed an interest in Big Foot Staffing and asked me how much I wanted for it, because he was keen to get into staffing and he recognised mine was a good business. I had a think and I told him, '$400,000', which was a basic multiplier calculation based on the revenue at the time and which wasn't unreasonable. He too thought it sounded fair but I don't think he had that kind of capital at that moment so he proposed a buy-out over time and he came up with a spreadsheet which showed how he would take over bit by bit while still needing my help to run the business until he was ready, and he's a great guy, so I agreed, 'Yeah, OK, we'll do that.' That should have been a weight off my shoulders, and moving back to Bend, and out of Portland, was certainly the right move, but I think, looking back, that a feeling of failure was beginning to nag at me. I looked at creating some other businesses, to capitalise on the money I had made and to make use of my entrepreneurial side, but none of them really panned out, so that would have added to the general malaise in my life at the time. As I've said, big single moments of pressure don't tend to get to me but it was like death by a thousand cuts, just failing, failing, failing. My relationship with Justine was not getting better. The drinking – by both of us - was not stopping so, that felt like another failure. Added to that, the one person in my life who I loved more than any other was growing away from me. Calvin was coming of age just as my relationship with Justine was getting bumpy, and while he was getting big and getting strong and feeling his testosterone, I was being too much of a domineering father, not least because of my hyper-vigilance. We were struggling because I wasn't letting loose of the reins to allow him to experience the pain of the world. I was acutely aware of his mother's issues, which had not gone away, and which affected him when he was living with her, and I didn't want him to have to experience the kind of pain I had had through my life so I was fighting tooth and nail against it, but the truth is that all young people need to experience it and to fail and to learn to succeed and all those things and I didn't recognise it at the time. More and more as he was growing and becoming a young man I still had my clamps in him and as he rebelled and we argued we would increasingly square up to each other during rows and on one occasion I hit him hard on the shoulder, much harder than I intended to, and it was a harbinger of things to come.

None of that seemed obvious to me as I jumped in my pick-up for the journey to the VA for my next annual doctor's check-up. Business was good, the partnership with Jeremy was going well and I should have been feeling fine but, though I couldn't put my finger on why, I guess I subconsciously knew I was not happy. Unknown to me, the dam holding back my emotions was failing badly. All it took for the dam to crumble was the simple question from Garnie-Jo: 'So how are you Ron?'

CHAPTER NINETEEN

Calvin's insolent shrug was like red rag to a bull and in that moment I lost it completely as the monster inside of me roared to the surface. I came around the kitchen counter, grabbed him by the shirt and slammed him back into the table and then I choke slammed him. He was already a big kid and growing stronger by the day, but I'm a pretty strong human and I dragged him into the living room, put him in a headlock and slammed him down on the ground. As he lay there, shocked, I hurled all sorts of vile expletives at him, letting him know in no uncertain terms how unhappy I was with him. My teenage son. The person I loved most in the world. I did that to him. And of all the things that I have done or had done to me in my life, since the incident in Germany, that was one of the hardest to come to terms with as I rightly suffered the fallout that followed. Things would only get worse before they got better, and they had already been pretty tough.

Days of tears and soul-searching had followed my breakdown at the VA clinic. Sure, I now had a PTSD diagnosis and I had finally realised the extent to which being raped as a teenager had wrecked my life, but it was only the beginning of a long road to some form of recovery and it was going to be a really rough road. I immediately began to grieve for the 35 wasted years when I had failed to speak up about what had happened to me; when I had failed to get help, when my corrosive secret had been eating me up from the inside. I mourned the broken relationships, the lost opportunities for real happiness, the harm I had done to others when a rage had been triggered.

THE MONSTER INSIDE OF ME

And the harm I had done to myself, year after year after year. I mourned the impulsiveness that had cost me so dear on so many occasions. I knew now that alcohol had not been the cure I was searching for, to end the torment I had failed to understand, but the catalyst for so many of my problems when paired with my PTSD. I decided immediately to stop drinking. I got super fit with CrossFit, which also gives me the endorphins I need to make me feel better about myself, and I lost about 40lbs with better food, diet and exercise, but not touching alcohol was not going to be a panacea for all my troubles. For a start, much of my relationship with Justine revolved around alcohol. Just because I had forsworn the booze did not mean that she was going to be able to stop. She tried, for my sake. She really did. A couple of times she agreed to quit but it didn't last very long and with her drinking came more rows, and I can't have been easy to live with at that time.

Once again I had been put on anti-depressants to try to help my mood and once again I had got off them as quickly as possible. The SSRIs – Selective Serotonin Reuptake Inhibitors – are a useful tool but my body does not tolerate them well. I lose my sex drive and I can't get very far from a toilet. I also view them as like alcohol or marijuana – just a mask for your problems. You are getting false serotonins in your head instead of doing things that really get you the pleasurable chemicals that you want and that you need. Producing genuine serotonins is the real way out of depression, but sobriety and abstaining from anti-depressants is a challenge because without the SSRIs you are going to have to sit with emotions that no one wants to sit with and come to terms with those emotions. No one wants to cry. No one wants to be angry. No one wants to be sad or sorrowful, but it is imperative to process those emotions as they come up and work towards finding inner peace. At least the help I was getting from VA psychiatrists and therapists was helping but that too was not without emotional pain. Talking about and writing down stuff that I had buried for 35 years, dragging it all back to the surface, was horrible and there were more tears. I'm prone to procrastination at the best of times but, man, would I procrastinate about writing down what I had been asked by the psychiatrists to remember because you're raking over some pretty negative times in your life and when you're processing PTSD you can link back so many of those negative points to where undiagnosed PTSD probably had a lot to do with it and that just makes you think, 'I wish I had done that better; I wish I had had the chance to do that better.' And not everyone I encountered during the process was there purely to help. My first psychological interview through the VA, to try to gauge my eligibility for disability benefits, was with a most unfriendly, unkind woman. You could absolutely tell her whole reason for being there was to try to deny me benefits and that in itself was really triggering. It angered me to my core. The trouble is that the system is set up to ferret out people who are faking it, right, or just trying to get something for nothing, and I understand that. I get that there are people out there who are trying it on, but I wasn't and nor are so many other veterans with PTSD, whether from combat or from MST or whatever, so why do we have to humiliate ourselves to get benefits that are available and that we deserve? I was initially granted 70 per cent disability, later raised to 100 per cent after numerous tests, but I had to jump through hoops and tell government agency after government agency what a piece of crap I am and that I am angry and that I get suicidal thoughts and that I have hurt people and that I still have thoughts of hurting people and why I am the way I am and it is totally dehumanizing. At the same time, however, every time I wrote down what I could remember, or when I told people what had happened to me, it seemed to help a little. You could see it in their faces when I told people that I know what I had gone through. Their jaws dropped. They were shocked, firstly that I was prepared to talk about it, secondly that it happens to the extent that it happens in the military, and thirdly that it had happened to me, of all people – sociable, kind, strong Ron who, ok, did sometimes have a bit of a temper! But every time I told people it gave me back a little bit of the power that had been taken away from me when I was raped.

That did not immediately make things any easier at home. On top of any difficulties Justine and I were having, the rows with Calvin were getting worse even though I was sober. By then his mother had kicked him out of her house and he was living with me full-time and while he was under my roof I felt responsible for making sure he did not fall into the same lifestyle his mother had had, and was still having, and that he could deal with her behaviour when he was exposed to it, because it could be pretty toxic. The fact was, however, that I was just too constraining and it took a horrific fall-out between me and Calvin for me to understand that. I organised for him to see this counsellor and we both met and interviewed with the guy and I was like, 'The whole reason I want Calvin to be here is I want him to learn some boundaries with his mother's behaviour so he can compartmentalize that and process that in a healthy way.' But what I found out is that in the state of Oregon, when you put your child in therapy, if they are 14 or older, you don't get to have any input with that therapist whatsoever. He will not divulge anything that is said between the two of them unless the child wants them to, and that infuriated me because it meant I had no way of making sure Calvin was getting the help I wanted him to get. So, two months into the therapy sessions, Calvin told me, 'I'm going to spend some time with my mom,' and that surprised me but my first question was, 'Have you done some boundaries work with your therapist about that, and what has that taught you?' and he had no answers. He just stood there in the kitchen, shrugging, his silence confirming he had not done the one thing I had asked him to do, and that triggered me and got me riled up, so I said, 'I don't think that's a good idea,' and that launched a whole new argument. I was right in the middle of starting my writing therapy, reliving what had happened to me in Germany and in the years since, and I was as raw as I've ever been in my life, so that anger was pretty easy to trigger, and that's when I grabbed Calvin and manhandled him to the floor in the living room. I can't remember what I said to him then but I certainly said some shitty things. When I let him up from the floor he was screaming at me, pissed, but mostly he was frightened. To my shame he was seriously scared - of his dad - and he wanted to leave. I wasn't having that so I took the keys to his car so he said, 'Fine, I'll walk,' and we had another awkward stand-off. Anyway, after a bit I gave him the keys to his car and I just let him go. Even then my anger was still simmering but as he left, I already felt terrible about what I had done. We kind of talked a day or two after that and it seemed that everything was OK between us, but then I lost it again for some reason. I don't even remember what it was about the next time but it would have been something trivial that certainly did not warrant the outburst it provoked from me and he basically shut me out of his life for a long while after that. It didn't help that his mother – paragon of virtue that she was – turned me in to child protection services. I then had a visit from the sheriff and charges were pressed. I had to submit to a number of interviews and an anxious wait before child protection services found me to be abusive but the sheriff did not. Unfortunately, it was a case of a stereotypical arsehole father clashing with a young teenager trying to become a man and I handled it really poorly. I had no excuses but I would rather have suffered a sanction under the law than the cold shoulder from my son, but that's what I got.

Now I needed Justine more than ever but drink was still a problem between us. We had been together, on and off, for five years and she hung in there for a while after my diagnosis but, understandably, I think it scared her. I think my reaction to it scared her and things got more difficult. Not having alcohol was the thing that was going to keep me alive; not drinking was what I needed to stop me losing control and killing myself, but it wasn't just about me. I didn't want to lose Justine but I knew if I quit drinking, as I had, and she didn't, then it just wasn't going to work between us. Even before my diagnosis there had been so many problems caused by our drinking and unless that ended, none of that stuff was going to be good. We were having yet another argument one time after she had been drinking and I finally said, 'Look, I need you to just shut your mouth!' I was actually pretty rude but we knew each other well enough that I needed to cut through the argument and make my point. She stopped shouting for a moment and I softened my stance too. 'Sometimes I'm just going to need to talk to you and vent out my problems,' I said, trying to explain how I was struggling to deal with what I was going through since my diagnosis. 'I'm going to need you just to kiss my forehead and tell me everything will be OK,' but she could not do that and not many days later she left and I was on my own again.

It certainly didn't feel like it then, but new purpose, new love, better times and, most of all, hope were waiting around the corner.

CHAPTER TWENTY

There were around 25 of us in the class, in a room provided for us by Bend High School, and as I took a first look around I was almost brought to tears trying to acclimatize to why we were all there. A couple of people I had known for some time noticed me struggling and came over to give me a hug and to ask me if I was OK, 'Not really,' I told them honestly, and they smiled an acknowledgement that also signalled they were there for me if I needed them and that comforted me. I glanced again to take in my surroundings. It felt strange to be in the buildings of the high school that was the arch cross-town rival when I was a teenager, though the video screens, computers and other IT stuff in the room made it very different to my high school days and quickly dragged me back to the brutal present. Around me were a number of mental health professionals, including those leading the class, and they were wonderful people, but the rest were mainly veterans. It was, after all, designed to be a veteran-focussed couple of days, which is what had attracted the sponsorship of some corporate donors, and that was cool. There were a few more faces I recognised, but plenty I didn't. There were some combat veterans who, during introductions, volunteered that they had PTSD and expressed their suicidal ideation. There were female veterans too, some who had suffered MST and some, that I knew, who had struggled. There were no other male MST victims apart from me or, at least, none who expressed it, which sadly came as no surprise. One woman, poor lady, would go on to have a complete mental breakdown as the nature of the Suicide Prevention class became too much for her, but these lessons were not about stopping us from killing ourselves. This was about us learning how to stop others taking their own lives. What we were taught was kind of immediate intervention stuff. How, when confronted with someone considering taking their own life, to keep them alive for five minutes; to keep them alive for ten minutes; to keep them talking long enough to get them professional help. We did role playing, with a partner, and it was really hard to do, really triggering, but by the second day of the class I felt more able to help someone if I needed, and that fitted well with my new purpose in life, to reach out to other victims of MST, particularly men, and those suffering PTSD, and try to get them to get help rather than taking their own lives. The thought did strike me that I myself had never knowingly reached out when I was at that point and I think that's how too many men are. They decide to do it and they do it. There is not a lot of reaching out and that is the importance of awareness and why I want to get a message to male victims of MST like me.

The fact is that I am lucky that my suicidal thought did not lead to my death and I have much to be grateful for. I am even grateful that what happened to me happened in the military. That might sound odd, and of course I wish that the rape had never happened, but there is help and there are benefits available for veterans that many people outside the military who suffer sexual trauma, and perhaps PTSD, might not so easily get. I have great therapists who are helping me now and, with their guidance, I am trying to build a new relationship with a better understanding of how previous relationships have brought me down. The thing is, I love to help other people. I would give my last dime to someone, and that's probably a bi-product of my PTSD. It's like, helping other people is what makes me feel good but, as my therapist pointed out, I don't help myself. I drain my cup until it's completely empty and then I want to kill myself, and when I do eventually fill my cup back up, as soon as it's full, I give it away again. To do anything else has always felt selfish but I need to work on loving myself and keeping energy for myself, apologising when I need to but expressing my intent and letting other people process their own thoughts and emotions, rather than me taking on their issues myself.

Along with the failure of my relationship with Justine, and losing my home and my suicide attempt, the worst error I ever made was to screw up so horrifically with Calvin and that was really hard because he is the thing I love most on the face of this world. It took a year – or close to a year – for him to come back to me and I thank God that he did. I have apologised numerous times and told him he didn't deserve what I did. Even though he hadn't done what I asked him to do, physically grabbing him was not a solution. Unfortunately I was in the middle of dealing with my PTSD and I reacted really inappropriately, but even having PTSD was not an excuse and I have told him that, and that's the premise on which we move forward. I think he now has a better understanding of what I have gone through and was going through but he also knows it was not right and it's still not OK. We've had a few screaming matches since – not recently because we have hashed it out – but I have told him, 'Look, I want you to be under my roof because if you are not you are going to struggle way harder, financially, but if I can't still be a father, if you can't respect me and my rules, which aren't that many, and I'm paying for everything, then you are going to have to go out in the world and do it on your own and that's not what I want, but there are some rules and there are some boundaries. You do need to respect me as your father, even though I have messed up. I have done my best to make amends for that and I always will, but you have to toe some lines yourself, as a son,' and I think he understands that better now, so the last year has been pretty darn good and I have been better at bringing stuff up in a non-threatening or argumentative way. I've also had the privilege of getting to know my daughter, Lindsie, a bit better but she and I have a very delicate relationship that isn't close. I've been lucky enough to have been involved in Calvin's life since the very beginning and that's been wonderful and the greatest gift to me, so the fact that I wasn't there for Lindsie, and didn't make that decision to be there for her, has always left me wondering if it could have been different and would have been different if she had had a direct fatherly influence from me. I did meet her when she was ready and took loads of photos of us when she was young, with my family and different things, especially when I would visit her or at Christmas time, but that was just Disneyland dadding; that's not being a parent; that's not being a father and I still have guilt over that, I really do, but I have come to terms with it. I think she tried to get close but I don't think she likes the kind of advice that I give and she probably thinks that I don't deserve to be a dad who gives advice and she's probably right, but I've lived a lot of life and learned some pretty hard lessons and I'm not a person that is going to reserve my opinions on how to succeed in life to someone who is an offspring.

Telling my story and determining to reach out to other male MST victims has also given me a reason to carry on and something to concentrate on, because it is so important. We have got to stop young men killing themselves over something that wasn't their fault or suffering blighted lives, as I have, because of their decision not to seek help or to speak out about what has been done to them. And yet…

The Suicide Prevention class was an eye-opener. It was really well delivered and very much in line with what I want to do with the rest of my life, reaching out to serving men and male veterans who have suffered MST, but as I sat there over two days of lessons I felt a fraud. How, I wondered, could I contemplate trying to help other people to not take their lives when I roll around that way, far too often? I am a person that still walks around with suicidal and homicidal thoughts and I have those thoughts in my head far more frequently than the average person. Here I am, trying to help other people and yet I'm in my own head all the time thinking about whether life is worth living. Today, resoundingly, it's yes, but I still have days where it's like, 'Fuck, it would just be easier to check out,' and I think that's a combination of the military – and especially the infantry – and the trauma experience of my rape which just made me feel like I don't value my life and it's been that way for more than 35 years. I also felt a fraud because there were combat vets in the class with PTSD and my story of PTSD through MST always makes me feel less than them. It feels to me like their PTSD, brought about through combat, is almost a badge of honour on their chest. I feel terrible for them, because they are going through, and have gone through, the same hell as me, but I feel like at least they can feel decent about themselves, like, 'At least this happened to me in war and I was doing what I thought was the right thing.' But when it comes to me expressing my story it is different. There is no machismo to it. MST feels like a shameful secret, but it shouldn't be. I wonder if that is why Vietnam veterans perhaps had so much trouble coming back to the US after the war, a lot of them with PTSD, because so many people, including themselves, did not think what they were doing was the right thing. But what happened to them was not their fault and what happened to me was not my fault and I should not have to bear the shame and nor should other men who have suffered MST. I wish that veterans and those still in the military who suffer from PTSD got more help and, when we're talking about the military, PTSD can come from all sorts of things, but at the moment, combat PTSD is really understandable to the public while PTSD through MST is not, and that has to change. When you look at Vet Centres around the USA, and there are thousands of them, one of their primary aims is to provide counselling services to veterans and as my therapist, who has worked in this field for years, has told me, there are all sorts of women's groups, but there are absolutely zero male MST groups. You can find MST stories from women but you can't find them from men because men won't talk about it, and that too has to change and that is what has given me a new purpose in life. I need to reach out to males victims of MST and get them to stop killing themselves.

In Bend alone, in a city of just 100,000, my therapist deals with five male MST victims and she has dealt with many others, yet I am the only one she has ever met in her career who has been prepared to talk about it. And, yes, recently I really stumbled. I really got depressed and got suicidal ideation thoughts, like, 'I'm worthless, I feel like shit.' Like, 'God! I can't even get any veterans to talk to me,' and it's frustrating but they just don't want to. Many are at least brave enough to get into therapy about it and they have been in therapy about it for a long time, but they haven't said a word to anyone else outside of therapy – probably even their own wives, or lovers, or friends or family. It's like the shame of it. I know. I get it. I buried it so deep I forgot about it for 35 years. I just thought I had some sociopathic freak inside of me. And, you know, it's been difficult to express my story, and to share my story but it has also lifted a lot of weight off my shoulders – the weight of the world, to be honest. I do gain my power back when I share my story, and I think that's the lesson for these men.

You know, the last twelve months have been a year of tremendous growth for me, not wanting to be on anti-depressants but wanting to learn so that I can help others. It's been hard, that's for sure, and I don't know if it's ever going to get super easy and that someday I'll be on Easy Street, full of bliss and joy, but if I could have some impact before I die; if I could achieve something that I personally see as profound, then I think that will help a ton. You, know, that's the juice. That's what's going to make my life better – and other people's lives better. I'm meeting more and more people who are MST victims like me but too many of them never get away from the victim mentality. I think that's why a lot of people turn to weed, or drinking, or anti-depressants, just to mask the pain. They hide from and don't confront the painful emotions – and I didn't for 35 years – but the painful emotions have to be confronted at some point or they never go away. Even confronting them, they never go away fully, so you have to teach your brain, your consciousness, your enlightenment to create an internal dialogue so that when your brain is telling you, 'You're a piece of shit. You're worthless' – and it does, often, especially in depression – then you can use your own dialogue: 'I'm advocating, I'm helping people, I am a good person, I am worthy of love and what that person did to me I had absolutely no part in it.' You have to get almost a mantra in your head of those things to convince yourself, and when you're successful in doing that then life gets better and you're not a victim any longer. And I am getting better and I am not a victim any more, and I am determined to help others so that they are not victims any more either. Every day I'm looking to heal and to better myself and then hopefully teach other people so that they don't have to suffer every damn day of their life or, worse, kill themselves.

AFTERWORD

I can't pretend it's been easy telling my story, revisiting some very painful memories and emotions – not just about the incident in Germany when I was a young, 19-year-old soldier but from the many years since. Has it helped? It has certainly helped me to address some serious issues in my life. Will it help others? I certainly hope so. That is my mission now. I know that I am one of the only men in the world admitting to being raped by another man in the military and I just know that sharing that story and being normal with that story is the only way I am going to get through to other men. But they are not easy to reach. I certainly wasn't and I am the first to admit that I am not at the end of my own journey, though things are going OK at the moment.

It's very much one step at a time, finding out what works and what doesn't; what helps and what doesn't. I recently tried Psilocybin treatment (psychedelic mushrooms), which is legal in Oregon. It's a natural therapy which I received through an accredited wellness center, registered with the state, and it was professionally administered under strict protocols and it felt like I was communicating with God - or the universe, or whatever you want to call it - through my subconscious. There is a lot of literature about it these days and there is some evidence of more success for some PTSD sufferers with Psilocybin than with talk therapies. The fact is that with PTSD we have got to rewire the brain away from automatic trigger responses that are linked to hyper-vigilance and get the brain to follow new neural pathways and that's what I think that trips into the subconscious can do for you. I certainly felt that it worked for me but it wasn't like I was just doing magic mushrooms for the sake of a wild ride with pretty lights. It's certainly not fun. It's frightening and there was a lot of crying. There was a lot of laughter too but it's definitely raw emotion and it's not easy. I was exhausted for two days afterwards; literally exhausted because you spend five, six, seven hours tense and crying and travelling around in your head, you know, wrestling with the stuff you have to wrestle with. I felt like I was shown the universe and its power and its vastness and then I was shown, way off in the distance, far back in a timeline, my very small pin-head trauma. To me, God's message was that my trauma is insignificant and it's in the past and that's where it should be and that was really powerful to me. I also learned about the divine feminine within all of us and that it never leaves us and that was hard for me to grapple with. When, during my mental breakdown, I told Stacy that I was exhausted from fighting, I think that fighting the divine feminine is what I have been doing my whole adult life since I was raped; being defensive; being hyper-vigilant; being reactive; thinking I've got to fight everything and the truth is I don't have to fight everything and that was probably the most poignant lesson of this experience. I definitely don't have to fight femininity within me or within anyone else that I encounter. I can learn patience. I can learn loving. I can learn to not take people's words personally and it's OK.

I think the Psilocybin treatment worked for me but I would not have done it if I had not done three years of other therapies first. I have done written therapy, I have done EMDR (Eye Movement Desensitization Reprocessing), CBT (Cognitive Behavioral Therapy) and every other type of talk therapy. I had a life coach for a year, too, and I have done all of these things not only to help myself but so that I can try to help other people understand what might work best for them. I have been on anti-depressant SSRIs (Selective Reuptake Inhibitors) and I did not like them but, you know, if someone is where I was, initially, then maybe they need to be on those for three to six months, or something like that, just to get to a headspace that is calm. Far more helpful to me was just quitting drinking and getting healthy and let's not forget about the benefits of exercise and about the right diet. They helped me and, yes, the talk therapies helped me too. There is no quick fix, and I would certainly not go to someone who is in the throes of a real mental breakdown and say, 'Hey, go do Psilocybin treatment!' I think you have got to get to a better place before you jump into that and I have got to a better place and that's where all the signs were leading me. When I was coming to the end of almost three years of talk therapies there was still stuff nagging at me and it was because I hadn't released it from within me. I'm trying to do that, and I felt that the Psilocybin treatment helped, but I don't think that work ever ends, to be honest. I'll certainly stay in touch with my other therapists and if I need to get back into that, on a monthly or weekly basis, I will, and I thank God for the VA affording me that luxury.

The fact is that there are thousands of veterans out there who are suffering, because MST = PTSD, and they need help. I have set up a website – www.MSTequalsPTSD.com - to point them in the right direction and I will keep trying to help by telling my story, even if I am a lone voice. It's kind of poignant to me that I have lost a lot of male friends over this which reinforces to me how they probably need to get help. Men don't want to confront fears or emotions and things that might make them cry but sometimes you have to, in order to put them right. I have certainly learned that I didn't have any part in what was done to me and that I need to forgive myself and I am doing that.

Right now, I'm in a good frame of mind. I just want other men who suffer MST to get to that place too.

APPENDIX I

A brief timeline of Military Sexual Trauma research.

Sexual assaults in the military are not a new phenomenon, even if the current term - Military Sexual Trauma – is a modern one. Serious attempts to address the epidemic of MST, however, are only relatively recent. Action to address the issue really started in earnest in the late 1980s to early 1990s but, as worthy as those efforts were, and have been since, and depending on what calculations are used, they do not seem to be working. MST is still happening on an appalling scale. So what are the military and the politicians missing?

1992.
Congress required the Department of Defence (DoD) to take action to try to stop sexual harassment and sexual assault in the military. The Department of Veterans Affairs (VA) was also required by congress to provide treatment to serving personnel and veterans experiencing the emotional and physical results of sexual violence suffered during their service. That's when the VA adopted the term Military Sexual Trauma to cover the psychological trauma resulting from sexual assault, battery or harassment. Like far too many young men who don't report MST, that was little help to me. By then I had been out of the military for a couple of years, still trying to bury any memory of what I had suffered and still afraid that if I reported my MST

and I was portrayed by my attackers (in my chain of command) to have been gay in the military I could be stripped of all benefits that I was entitled upon my honourable discharge, and perhaps even retrospectively punished. The Don't Ask Don't Tell policy introduced by the Clinton administration in 1993 did absolutely nothing to allay those fears and that unhelpful policy would exist for the next 17 years.

2004.

It would be another decade before the DoD established the Sexual Assault Prevention and Response Office (SAPRO) to examine MST in the military, to come up with prevention efforts, to provide more medical care and support for survivors and to improve the accountability both of the military and individual perpetrators. Meanwhile, veterans were still dying by their own hands, and there were no figures on how many of them might have suffered MST.

2014.

Increased research into military suicides does not seem to have been matched by research into MST and it would be another ten years before a major independent assessment of sexual assault, sexual harassment and gender discrimination in the military by the RAND Corporation National Defence Research Institute. Meanwhile, growing support from the VA for vulnerable veterans did not extend to those who submitted compensation claims for sexual assaults during their military service. Most were denied benefits, though more recently the VA has begun to grant claims for MST at an increasing rate. From 2011 to 2021 the number of MST claims filed to the VA by men would rise more than 119 per cent, from 1,357 to 2,969.

The 2014 RAND report, based on a study of data on 560,000 US service members, found that one in 20 women (4.9%) and one in 100 men (1%) on active duty experienced a sexual assault in the year of the survey. Further, more than one in four women

(26%) and more than one in fourteen men (7%) on active duty experienced sexual harassment or gender discrimination. It also found that rates for sexual assault among women in the military was similar to the chance of civilian women suffering a sexual assault – around 16.6% - but, crucially, for civilian women that was over a life-time while, for military women, it was during their period of service (typically two to six years). The report highlighted how MST tends to happen early in the military career. As I had found, the predators don't pick on those of their own age, rank or status, but the vulnerable younger members – the poorer, less well educated members of society that the military recruits from, and the very people they should be caring for. The RAND study found that more than 80% are victimized between the ages of 17 and 24. And while women reported a greater risk of falling victim to MST, the vastly greater ratio of men in the military meant the numbers of male and female victims were comparable. Of the 20,300 military members who reported experiencing a sexual assault in the year before the survey, the RAND survey found more than 10,600 were men and more than 9,600 were women. And that was just from those who were willing to admit it. It found the DoD only received one report of assault from a serviceman for every four reports from servicewomen. The RAND study also found male survivors of sexual assault were more likely to have experienced multiple assaults, to have suffered 'gang rape' with assaults by multiple attackers, and to report the incident as part of 'hazing' or 'initiation ceremonies', motivated by abuse and humiliation and, too often, they did not perceive these assaults as 'sexual', though very often they were.
2015.
A year later the DoD confirmed 6,083 reports of sexual assault and 657 formal complaints of sexual harassment, though, as the RAND Military Workplace Study (RMWS) had previously

shown, only a limited number of service personnel who suffer MST (particularly among men) actually report it. The same year the DoD announced a plan to prevent and respond to sexual assault of military men, but admitted: "Our knowledge about male sexual assault, in both the military and civilian sectors, is lacking due to the scarce number of men who report the crime and the limited research on male incidence." It was estimated that about 38 per cent of women reported when they suffered MST, compared to only 10 per cent of men. The Department said: "One theory as to why males may choose not to report a sexual assault is they fear disbelief, blame and scorn if they choose to report." It said that the Department had taken steps to enhance prevention efforts throughout the military, improve response services and increase outreach to men. As an example, it said the Services and National Guard Bureau (NGB) then included male-specific scenarios and information about sexual assault disguised as hazing or bullying and other abusive or humiliating acts in their sexual assault prevention training. It said the Department had sought expert assistance, conducted research and applied the data it had collected to inform practices that addressed male sexual assault. It admitted: "Despite these efforts, male reporting remains low and knowledge about the best methods to promote reporting among males is limited. It said it would convene a group of research specialists from the DoD, SAPRO, the Services, the NGB, the Service Surgeons General, Office of the Assistant Secretary of Defence for Health Affairs, Office of Diversity Management and Equal Opportunity and others, to develop a unified communication plan to reach out to military men, to improve the understanding of sexual assault on men among male military members, to ensure support services met the needs of male survivors of MST and to develop metrics to assess how efforts to prevent and respond to male MST were doing.

2018.
A 2018 study of active-duty, reserve and National Guard personnel still reported an overall lack of awareness of sexual assault of men in the military. It further found an inclination to blame or marginalize male victims and that the barriers to reporting sexual assault included stigma, a lack of confidence in leadership and feeling 'trapped' by the physical confines of deployment.

2019.
A report by the VA's Rocky Mountain Mental Illness Research, Education and Clinical Center in Colorado also found under-reporting of MST among men and that it might 'derive from men's concerns about stigma, shame, rape myths, lack of past empathic response to disclosures of MST and the perceived implications of reporting MST for one's masculinity and sexuality'. It found that, for the same reasons, male MST survivors were at 'elevated risk for a vast array of adverse health outcomes', including depression, anxiety, nightmares, flashbacks, Post-Traumatic Stress Disorder, anger management issues, self-blame and low self-esteem.

The problem of MST is, of course, not unique to the US military. A Review into Inappropriate Behaviour in the UK Armed Forces by Air chief Marshal Michael Wigston in July 2019, following media reports of an alleged sexual assault on a 17-year-old trainee, concluded that the UK Armed Forces suffered unacceptable levels of sexism, racism and bullying because it was led by 'a pack of white middle-aged men'. It found that sexual assaults and sexual harassment remained a serious issue in spite of efforts there to prevent and respond to it. Just as in the US, the problems were exacerbated by the chain of command having jurisdiction over allegations of sexual assault. The British Ministry of Defence (MoD) found that some matters that started out as an allegation of sexual assault were being reduced to a lesser charge so that they could be dealt with summarily by a Commanding Officer, rather than by the Director of Service Prosecutions who had to deal offences covered by the British Sexual Offences Act 2003. Moreover, while the Royal Military Police were investigating significant numbers of rape cases which were increasing year on year, the conviction rates were negligible. Of the 48 rape cases that got to court martial in 2017, just two resulted in a conviction; The following year, just ten rape cases got to court martial, with just three convictions; In 2019, 15 rape cases got to court martial, with just three convictions; and in 2021, 25 rape cases would get to court martial, with just six convictions. Over the course of the five years, the contested conviction rate (at court martial) averaged just 14%, but that was just the cases that got to court martial. In the UK civilian justice system, by comparison, the conviction rate in 2022 was 62%, though only 5% of rape allegations got to court, so just a 3% conviction rate for those civilian rape cases where the victim even made a complaint, and a much worse conviction rate for the military.

2020.

In the US, the Pentagon noted that survivors of MST, male and female, were often reluctant to report their trauma for reasons including a desire to move on, to maintain privacy and to avoid feelings of shame, but that when they did report they often found that the military culture and the command structure did not take their allegations seriously and that the military justice system provided little accountability. According to the 2020 statistics, just 225 of 5,640 eligible cases of non-consensual sexual offenses went to court martial and only 50 of those resulted in a conviction. That's a 22% contested conviction rate, but represents a 0.88% conviction rate for all allegations. A VA spokesman at the time said that the effect of poor accountability and the sense of shame can continue well beyond the victim's period of military service and he said: "Despite successes in ensuring access to care for men who experienced MST, ongoing stigma related to experiencing sexual trauma in men also may be a barrier to seeking care." A report carried on The Hill political website in 2019, by Kayla Williams, a Senior Fellow and Director of the Military, Veterans and Society Program at the Center for a New American Security, had suggested that men who filed a claim for PTSD with the VA, as a result of MST, were being systematically discriminated against by the Veterans Benefits Administration (VBA), in spite of improvements to the claims processing system to try to reduce the stark disparities that had been identified between the rate of claims granted when the cause of PTSD was MST compared to other events, such as combat. Kayla Williams pointed out that the changes, over seven years, had largely eliminated the gap and that PTSD claims granted for MST-related causes had climbed 20% from 35.6% in 2011 (26.9% for men) to 56.6% in 2018, while the rate for PTSD claims due to causes other than MST had remained unchanged at around 54% over the same time. But she found that the grant rate for men (44.7%) had lagged significantly behind the 57.7% rate for women. She concluded: "It is glaringly apparent that men's cases are not being handled equitably." I am glad to say that that was not the experience that I found and I have nothing but praise for the VA. The VA's Inspector General found in 2018 that thousands of MST survivors might have been incorrectly denied benefits due to paperwork and procedural mistakes and they made a series of recommendations, including that the VBA have specialized raters process MST claims.

2021.
President Joe Biden signed an executive order making sexual harassment a crime under US military law for the first time, and Congress passed significant military justice reforms that took away from the chain of command the role of deciding to

prosecute cases of sexual assault. It was hoped that that would prevent retaliation and lead more survivors to report sexual offences. President Biden also directed the DoD to establish a 90-day Independent Review Commission on Sexual Assault in the Military to assess the Department's efforts and make recommendations. As a result, the authors of a report in the National Library of Medicine - State of the Knowledge of VA Military Sexual Trauma Research - organised an overview of prevalence, adverse consequences and evidence-based treatments targeting the after-effects of MST. The Report found that, although not all MST survivors experience long-term adverse consequences, 'for many they can be significant, chronic and enduring and span mental and physical health outcomes as well as cumulative impairments in functioning.' It found that the consequences were similar to those suffered by victims of sexual trauma in other settings, such as interpersonal betrayal and victim-blaming, but with the addition of consequences unique to a military context, like fear of reprisals or ostracism, and having to work and live alongside a perpetrator. It found that the most common mental health impact was PTSD which often coincides with major depression, anxiety, eating disorders, substance use disorders and increased suicidality. Physical health consequences, it found, include greater chronic disease burden, such as hypertension, and impaired reproductive health and sexual functioning. For male survivors of MST, it found the stress suffered could be increased by gender-specific rape myths which, when male victims suppressed their emotions, was associated with more severe PTSD symptoms. Gender-specific rape myths include the false ideas that men cannot be raped because they are strong enough to defend themselves; men lie about being raped to cover up their sexual orientation; men seek violent relationships; men are not traumatized by rape; and that male rapists are homosexual. MST sufferers frequently reported that 'the military institution contributed to an environment in which MST was common, likely to occur and difficult to report.' The report added that fears of disruption in unit cohesion and implications for military careers were more deeply felt by male MST victims and went on: 'Survivors of MST may experience subsequent distrust of both comrades and command. The disintegration of the support structure in the military is uniquely egregious not only because the nature of the job requires trusting one another with one's very life, but also because military service includes working and living with one's fellow soldiers. Having to continue to work and live side by side with one's perpetrator and potentially rely on one's perpetrator for safety in life-threatening situations presents an environment from which escaping the effects of MST may be impossible. This context compounds distress and complicates later help-seeking.' Former US Marine Zachary Clayborne Dietrich, PsyD, a licenced psychologist at LifeStance Health, which provides virtual and in-person outpatient mental healthcare, similarly reported around the same time: "Often there is an additional layer to the event because the person who perpetrated the assault was supposed to be someone the victim could trust to protect their life."

2022.
A report in The Intercept online media outlet in November found more than 103,000 veterans, of all genders, were at that time formally recognized by the VA as having been sexually traumatized during their service. It described the sexual assault of one in four US servicewomen as an epidemic but said 'the sexual assault of men in the military is also widespread and vastly underreported.' It said that each day, on average, more than 45 men in the armed forces are sexually assaulted. For women, it is 53 per day, according to a Pentagon report from September 2022, but, as with previous research, the report

found that about 90 per cent of men in the military did not report a sexual assault they experienced in 2021 and about 71 per cent of women failed to report such an attack.

2023.

A 2021 Report – El Hombre Invisible by Tony Wright and Stuart Honor – published by the UK's Forward Assist charity in 2023, interviewed 30 male survivors of MST aged between 37 and 69. It found that only 25% reported their MST at the time it happened during their service, and those that did had very limited success in getting a resolution or sense that justice was served.

APPENDIX II

A brief timeline of veteran suicide research

If we look at the figures on suicides during and after military service, some researchers point to the fact that, before 2008, being in the military was actually some protection against suicide. They speculate that the camaraderie and the sense of purpose that came from being part of the military made men in the forces less likely than those in the general population to take their own lives. But that could not be said of veterans.

1958.
The first suicide prevention center in the United States was opened more than 60 years ago to address the issue of veteran suicides, which was a recognisable problem even then.

1990s.
It was not until the mid-90s, however, that a national strategy to tackle veteran suicides was developed, including several Congressional Resolutions.

2007.
The Joshua Omvig Veterans Suicide Prevention Act created a comprehensive program for dealing with the number of suicides, including outreach facilities at each Veterans Affairs Office and the launch of a 24-hour hotline – the Veterans Crisis Line. Since that time it has answered more than 4.4 million calls and emergency services have been dispatched to callers in crisis on more than 138,000 occasions.

2009.

The anonymous online chat service, launched two years later, has engaged in more than 500,000 chats.

2011.

The text-messaging service added in November 2011 has responded to more than 150,000 texts. But still the emphasis was on looking at combat-related PTSD, depression and survivors' guilt for reasons why veterans had difficulty in transitioning to civilian life. A surge in combat operations around that time helped to cement that thinking as suicide rates among veterans rose steadily.

2012.

In 2012, more active duty service members (177) died by suicide than were killed in combat (176), but even that figure was dwarfed by the estimated 7,500 veterans who killed themselves that year.

2013.

The VA released its much-quoted study into veteran suicides between 1999 and 2010 which showed that around 22 veterans a day were killing themselves. That's one every 65 minutes according to the figures which were based on data from veterans who used VA's Veterans Health Administration (VHA) services and from approximately three million mortality records obtained from the 20 states which would provide them. Further analysis that year found a suicide rate among veterans of around 30 per 100,000 population, per year, compared with a civilian rate of 14 per 100,000.

2015.

The Senate passed the Clay Hunt Veterans Suicide Prevention Act, requiring the Secretary of Veterans Affairs to organize an annual third-party evaluation of the VA's mental health care and suicide prevention programs, to mandate the VA to update details of its mental health care services on its website at least once every 90 days, and to offer educational incentives for psychiatrists who commit to serving in the VHA. It also required the VA to collaborate with non-profit mental health organizations to prevent veteran suicides, and to extend veterans' eligibility for VA hospital care, medical service care and nursing home care.

2016.

Another report, released by the VA in August 2016, was based on the nation's largest analysis of veteran suicides. Whereas the 2013 VA report was based only on data from veterans who used VHA services, or from limited mortality records, and amounted to approximately three million records, the new report reviewed more than 55 million veterans' records from 1979 to 2014 from every state. It still showed at least 20 veterans a day killing themselves.

2019.

The National Veteran Suicide Prevention annual Report released by the VA confirmed that there were 6,000 or more veteran suicides per year from 2008 to 2017 – more than 16-a-day. It also found that the suicide rate for veterans was 1.5 times the rate of non-veteran adults and that veterans, though they made up only 7.9% of the US adult population, accounted for 13.5% of all adult deaths by suicide in the US. In May that year, President Donald trump signed an executive order – the PREVENTS initiative – to try to counter veteran suicide. Previously, the VA and other federal agencies had relied on veterans to self-identify when needing help. The PREVENTS initiative secured $73.1 billion for veteran health services with the aim of equipping state and local governments with the resources needed to identify and intervene in scenarios where veterans might be at risk of suicide. That included $18.6 billion towards mental health services.

Separately, in November, the House of Representatives discussed a potential three-year program, backed by the VA, to give grants to local organizations that support veterans who it might have overlooked. This was because, statistically, 14 out of the estimated 20 veterans and serving military personnel a day who died from suicide at the time were not in regular communication with the VA, just like me when I first tried to kill myself. The idea, though it gathered bipartisan support, never got past Congress.

2020.

The VA reported a decrease in veterans' suicides, down 10% from a peak in 2018, but still more than double the rate of suicides among non-veteran adults in the US. The report showed that there had been a 9.7% decline in all veterans' suicides, in the two-year timescale, compared to a 5.5% drop in suicides in the general adult population, but that the suicide rate among post-9/11 veterans had continued to rise.

2021.

A 'Costs Of War' study by Brown University's Watson Institute of International and Public Affairs estimated that 30,177 veterans of post-9/11 conflicts had died by suicide – at least four times as many as the 7,057 active-duty personnel killed in the conflicts. A separate report the same year, by Thomas Howard Suitt at Boston University, found that suicide rates among the active military personnel and veterans of the post-9/11 conflicts had been climbing faster that the rates of suicide were increasing in the general public.

2022.

A new study – Operation Deep Dive, by America's Warrior Partnership – found that, on average, as many as 44 veterans a day die from suicide – 2.4 times greater than the official estimate - when accounting overlooked causes of death that are aligned with suicidal and self-harm behaviour. The study calculated there were 24 recorded suicides a day among veterans, and 20 deaths a day as a result of self-harm/accidents by veterans. A report the same year by the Iraq and Afghanistan Veterans of America found nearly half of US military service members had seriously considered suicide since joining the Armed Forces.

2023.
A study of 2.5 million service member records led by the University of Texas at San Antonio examined suicide among veterans of post-9/11 conflicts and found that the annual figures for suicides had increased since 2018 and had gone up more than tenfold from 2006 to 2020. It also found that the highest rates of veteran suicide were among those aged 35 to 44, those aged 25 to 34, Native Americans, Asian and Pacific Islanders, and, significantly, veterans with traumatic brain injuries. Veterans with such injuries had suicide rates 56% higher than those without a head injury and three times higher than the general population. Jeffrey Holland, an associate professor of public health at the University of Texas at San Antonio said of the findings: "We were pretty stunned, honestly. Even though this is just a descriptive analysis, the trends are so alarming we felt we needed to report it as soon as possible." The findings of the report built on work published the previous year by Professor Howard that found veterans with even mild traumatic brain injury were more likely to die by suicide, accidents or homicide than their counterparts who had never received blows to the head. What about the mental brain injury caused by MST, I wonder? The results, the report authors conceded, might have been skewed by failures to classify some deaths as suicide, the underreporting of traumatic brain injuries (TBI) and the fact that the research did not include veterans who left the service in less than three years or who had not received care at the VA. Professor Howard said current efforts to prevent

suicide in the military and veteran population 'do not appear to have impacted the trend.' He said: "I think this points to the need to re-evaluate how we are going about trying to reduce suicide. I think it is not solely a clinical solution, but there is a need for a much broader, multifaceted approach."

Separately, as of January 17, 2023, all US veterans are eligible to receive emergency mental health care at no cost. This applies even if the individual isn't enrolled in the VA system. The policy also includes the cost of ambulance rides, up to 30 days of inpatient care and up to 90 days of outpatient care.

MY CONCLUSIONS:

The enduringly high number of suicides by veterans, and the horrific scale of the MST suffered by service personnel, male and female, are both issues that should worry anyone who cares about our military community, both active duty and veterans, and I'm not convinced that enough research is going into possible links between the two problems, because it seems to me that the incidence of MST has got to be a component in the statistics on veteran suicide.

A 2022 study from the University of Manchester in the UK found that veterans there are at no greater risk of suicide than the general population, which is very much at odds with the situation in the US. I wonder if access to firearms - which are the most common method of suicide among US veterans - might be a big difference, since the legal ownership of firearms is very tightly controlled in the UK. That said, the University of Manchester study found that serving in the military for longer periods of time and serving on operational tours were actually associated with reduced suicide risk, while younger veterans and those who left after a short career were more at risk. It found that veterans over the age of 35 were at lower risk of suicide than the general population while younger veterans were at increased risk. Even though overall suicide risk was similar to the general population, the study found suicide rates were 2-4 times higher for veterans under the age of 25, when compared with the general population of the same age group. Again, that seems to conflict a little with a study done by the VA in the US which found that veterans are more likely to develop symptoms of PTSD for a number of reasons, such as longer times at war, lower levels of education, more severe combat conditions, other soldiers around them being killed, brain/head trauma, female gender, life-lasting physical injuries and military structure. The UK study, meanwhile, found that being male, being discharged from the forces before the age of 34, being untrained and having served for less than ten years were risk factors for suicide.

Looking at the results of previous studies, which found bullying, MST and other victimization was more likely to happen early in a soldier's career, leads me to wonder how many servicemen and women who were discharged from the forces before the age of 34 left because of unreported MST or bullying and, again, whether there is a link between veteran suicides and MST. Too many young veterans do not appear in the research findings because they were discharged from the military early and/or have not accessed the VA's VHA services. Without them coming forward to perhaps say that they suffered MST, and maybe that is why they left the service, we can't ever know how much they are at risk of suicide.

ABOUT THE AUTHOR

Ron Carter

Ron's time in the Army Infantry forged a deep sense of discipline and purpose that added to an already strong work ethic. Since leaving the Army he has enjoyed an eclectic mix of careers, including being the Lead Financial Advisor for a $4 billion bond portfolio. Nearly a decade in sales and sales management within the staffing industry revealed a real passion for empowering others to find pride and purpose in their work and, as the founder of Big Foot Staffing, he has pursued that mission with the same vigor he applied to his military service.

A loving father of two, and a cornerstone of a large extended family, Ron's dedication to helping veterans is profound and personal and he has set up the MST=PTSD website with a mission to support and advocate for those who have endured sexual trauma in the military.

ABOUT THE AUTHOR

Martin Phillips

Martin Phillips is a British Press Awards-nominated writer with more than 40 years' experience working in 'Fleet Street' for some of the biggest selling newspapers in the world. His long and varied career has seen him traveling the globe with members of the UK's Royal Family, conducting interviews with countless celebrities - from Hollywood greats to sporting superstars and military heroes – and reporting from war zones and natural disasters as well as covering stories from places as wide-ranging as the snow-covered Andes and the wreck of Titanic at the bottom of the Atlantic.

Martin, a father-of four, has ghost-written four books and is also a volunteer search and rescue technician who has deployed around the worldwith fellow humanitarians in the wake of disasters such as hurricanes and earthquakes.

Printed in Dunstable, United Kingdom